The PLC+ Bo

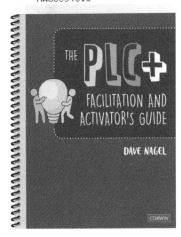

PLC+

Better Decisions and Greater Impact by Design

What's this book about?

- Provides a brief history of PLCs
- Introduces the PLC+ framework questions and crosscutting values
- Shows the PLC+ in action in various settings

When do I need this book?

- You want to understand the purpose of PLCs
- You want to learn a new framework for effective PLCs
- You want to reinvigorate and increase the impact of your existing PLC

The PLC+ Playbook

A Hands-On Guide to Collectively Improving Student Learning

What's this book about?

- Provides a practical, hands-on guide to implementing the full PLC+ cycle
- Guides PLC+ group members through 22 modules as they answer the five guiding questions and focus on the four crosscutting values
- Offers modules comprising array of tools that support implementation of the PLC+ framework

When do I need this book?

- You want to plan and implement the PLC+ framework in collaborative settings
- You want to implement the PLC+ model step by step in your own PLC

The PLC+ Facilitation and Activator's Guide

What's this book about?

- Provides guidance for the PLC+ team activators

When do I need this book?

- You are a PLC+ activator and want to do the best possible job for your group
- You are an activator and want to pre-plan the implementation of your PLC+
- You need help to guide the group in overcoming obstacles or having difficult conversations

PLC+

BETTER DECISIONS AND
GREATER IMPACT BY DESIGN

PLC+

BETTER DECISIONS AND GREATER IMPACT BY DESIGN

Douglas Fisher • Nancy Frey • John Almarode
Karen Flories • Dave Nagel

CORWIN

FOR INFORMATION:

Corwin

A SAGE Company

2455 Teller Road

Thousand Oaks, California 91320

(800) 233-9936

www.corwin.com

SAGE Publications Ltd.

1 Oliver's Yard

55 City Road

London EC1Y 1SP

United Kingdom

SAGE Publications India Pvt. Ltd.

B 1/I 1 Mohan Cooperative Industrial Area

Mathura Road, New Delhi 110 044

India

SAGE Publications Asia-Pacific Pte. Ltd.

18 Cross Street #10-10/11/12

China Square Central

Singapore 048423

Director and Publisher, Corwin Classroom: Lisa Luedeke

Editorial Development Manager: Julie Nemer

Senior Editorial Assistant: Sharon Wu

Production Editor: Melanie Birdsall

Copy Editor: Cate Huisman

Typesetter: C&M Digitals (P) Ltd.

Proofreader: Sarah J. Duffy

Indexer: Sheila Bodell

Cover Designer: Gail Buschman

Marketing Manager: Deena Meyer

Library of Congress Cataloging-in-Publication Data

Names: Fisher, Douglas, author.

Title: PLC+ : better decisions and greater impact by design / Douglas Fisher, Nancy Frey, John Almarode, Karen Flories, Dave Nagel.

Other titles: PLC plus

Description: Thousand Oaks, California : Corwin, 2019. | Includes bibliographical references and index.

Identifiers: LCCN 2019008221 | ISBN 9781544361796 (pbk. : alk. paper)

Subjects: LCSH: Professional learning communities. | Teachers—Professional relationships. | Teachers—In-service training.

Classification: LCC LB1731 .F4868 2019 | DDC 370.71/1—dc23

LC record available at https://lccn.loc.gov/2019008221

This book is printed on acid-free paper.

21 22 23 10 9 8 7

DISCLAIMER: This book may direct you to access third-party content via web links, QR codes, or other scannable technologies, which are provided for your reference by the author(s). Corwin makes no guarantee that such third-party content will be available for your use and encourages you to review the terms and conditions of such third-party content. Corwin takes no responsibility and assumes no liability for your use of any third-party content, nor does Corwin approve, sponsor, endorse, verify, or certify such third-party content.

CONTENTS

Visit the companion website at
resources.corwin.com/plcplus
for videos.

LIST OF VIDEOS

Note From the Publisher: The authors have provided video and web content throughout the book that is available to you through QR (quick response) codes. To read a QR code, you must have a smartphone or tablet with a camera. We recommend that you download a QR code reader app that is made specifically for your phone or tablet brand.

Videos may also be accessed at **resources.corwin.com/plcplus**

Video 1: An Introduction to PLC+

Video 2: Introduction to Chapter 1

Video 3: Introduction to Chapter 2

Video 4: Introduction to Chapter 3

Video 5: Introduction to Chapter 4

Video 6: Introduction to Chapter 5

Video 7: Introduction to Chapter 6

Video 8: Introduction to Chapter 7

ABOUT THE AUTHORS

Douglas Fisher, PhD, is Professor of Educational Leadership at San Diego State University and a leader at Health Sciences High and Middle College. He has served as a teacher, language development specialist, and administrator in public schools and nonprofit organizations, including 8 years as the Director of Professional Development for the City Heights Collaborative, a time of increased student achievement in some of San Diego's urban schools. Doug has engaged in Professional Learning Communities for several decades, building teams that design and implement systems to impact teaching and learning. He has published numerous books on teaching and learning, such as *Developing Assessment-Capable Visible Learners* and *Engagement by Design*. He can be reached at dfisher@sdsu.edu.

Nancy Frey, PhD, is a Professor of Educational Leadership at San Diego State University and a leader at Health Sciences High and Middle College. She has been a special education teacher, reading specialist, and administrator in public schools. Nancy has engaged in Professional Learning Communities as a member and in designing schoolwide systems to improve teaching and learning for all students. She has published numerous books, including *The Teacher Clarity Playbook* and *Rigorous Reading*. She can be reached at nfrey@sdsu.edu.

John Almarode, PhD, is an Associate Professor of Education at James Madison University, the Co-Director of the Center for STEM Education Outreach and Engagement, and the Director of the Content Teaching Academy. Prior to his work with schools, he served as a mathematics and science teacher in Virginia. John has engaged in professional learning with teachers and instructional leaders across the globe, integrating the science of how we learn into classrooms in all content areas and across all grade levels. He has published numerous books on teaching and learning, such as *Clarity for Learning* and *From Snorkelers to Scuba Divers.* He can be reached at almarojt@jmu.edu.

Karen Flories, MS Ed, is a full-time Professional Learning Consultant for Corwin and works with teachers and leaders across the nation. Prior to her role with Corwin, Karen was the Executive Director of Educational Services and Director of Literacy and Social Studies in Valley View School District, after serving as the English Department Chair for Romeoville High School. Karen's classroom experience includes high school English, special education, and alternative education. She has co-authored several books, including student learner notebooks on *Becoming an Assessment-Capable Visible Learner* for Grades 3–5 and 6–12. She can be reached at karen .flories@corwin.com.

Dave Nagel, MS Ed, is a full-time Professional Learning Consultant with Corwin. Dave has been a professional developer both nationally and internationally since 2003, working deeply with schools in the areas of assessment, improved grading and feedback actions to promote student learning, instructional leadership, and effective collaboration focused on ensuring both student and adult learning. Dave has done significant research related to effective collaboration and has developed practical instruments to assist collaborative teams in monitoring their adult behaviors to ensure having an effective team. In addition to his professional development work with teachers, leaders, community members, and other stakeholders, Dave is also a frequent speaker at state and national conferences and has contributed to several books, including *Effective Grading Practices for Secondary Teachers,* and published articles. He can be reached at dave.nagel@corwin.com.

ACKNOWLEDGMENTS

REVIEWERS

Dan Alpert
Program Director and
  Publisher, Equity and
  Professional Learning
Corwin
San Francisco, CA

Janice Bradley
Assistant Director, Utah
  Education Policy Center
University of Utah
Salt Lake City, UT

Amy Colton
Executive Director and
  Senior Consultant
Learning Forward
  Michigan
Ann Arbor, MI

Jenni Donohoo
Author and Professional
  Learning Facilitator

Carol Flenard
Assistant Superintendent
  of Instruction
Spotsylvania County
  Public Schools
Fredericksburg, VA

Constance Hamilton
Author, Consultant, and
  Curriculum Director
Saranac Community
  Schools
Caledonia, MI

PLC+ ADVISORY BOARD

Allen Aida
Teacher/Program Manager
Health Sciences High and
Middle College

Dan Alpert
Program Director and
Publisher, Equity and
Professional Learning
Corwin

Ben Allred
Director of High Schools
and ESL
Cabarrus County Schools

Olivia Amador
Professional Learning
Consultant
Corwin

Morcease Beasley
Superintendent
Clayton County
Public Schools

Elizabeth Cardenas-Lopez
Director of Literacy
Evanston/Skokie School
District 65

Amy Colton
Executive Director
Learning Forward Michigan

Benjamin P. Edmondson
Executive Vice President
HighScope Educational
Research Foundation

Carol Flenard
Assistant Superintendent
of Instruction
Spotsylvania County
Public Schools

Constance Hamilton
Author, Consultant, and
   Curriculum Director
Saranac Community Schools
Caledonia, MI

Sonja Hollins-Alexander
Director of Professional
   Learning
Corwin

Billy Ray Jones
Supervising Principal,
   South Jones High School
   7–12, Jones County
   School District

Cathy Lassiter
Professional Learning
   Consultant
Corwin

Stanley Law
Principal, Arlington
   Community High School
Indianapolis Public Schools

Lisa Luedeke
Director and Publisher
Corwin Literacy

Tricia McManus
Assistant Superintendent of
   Educational Leadership and
   Professional Development
Hillsborough County Public
   Schools

Deena Meyer
Executive Marketing Manager
Corwin

Vicki Park
Assistant Professor of
   Educational Leadership
San Diego State University

Lisa Shaw
Senior Vice President and
    Managing Director, US
Corwin

Tyra Shearn
Editorial Director
Corwin

Dominique Smith
Chief of Educational
    Services and Teacher
    Relations
Health Sciences High and
    Middle College

Julie Smith
Senior Director, Global
    Visible Learning
Corwin

Tommy Thompson
Principal
New London High School

Vania Tiatto
Director of Professional
    Learning, Australia
Corwin

Debra White
School Improvement Specialist
Georgia Department of
    Education

James Wright
Assistant Professor of
    Educational Leadership
San Diego State University

INTRODUCTION

"I have a PLC team meeting today."

That statement conjures up a range of responses among administrators and teachers. Each of us has likely been part of a PLC in some way, shape, or form. Our experiences in those PLCs may have been good, bad, or ugly. You may have wondered to yourself: *What am I supposed to get out of this meeting? What does this have to do with me and my teaching? Aren't there better uses of my time?* We fully recognize that although most PLCs have noble intentions, there is a need to remedy some of the dysfunction that, at times, makes its way into a PLC structure and thus hinders the impact the PLC can potentially have on learning—our own learning as well as that of our students.

Lots of educational terms are introduced into our profession, and over time, many of them are watered down, are misused, or eventually lose their meaning altogether. *Professional learning communities* is just such a term. One of the biggest hinderances to the impact the PLC can have on teaching and learning is the misconception about the intention and implementation of PLCs. So, to clear up any misunderstandings, let's start off by exploring what PLCs are *not*. We'll call them the myths of PLCs. Maybe you have seen or experienced something on this list:

Video 1
An Introduction to PLC+

resources.corwin.com/plcplus

To read a QR code, you must have a smartphone or tablet with a camera. We recommend that you download a QR code reader app that is made specifically for your phone or tablet brand.

- **The PLC Book Club.** Reading a book or article together as a staff can be a fun and even enlightening experience, but doing so does not make a PLC. In a PLC, groups of teachers may choose to learn more and read something in common, but that occurs only when they are in search of an answer to a specific question (what we call a common challenge) they have crafted about moving the learning of their students forward. Unfortunately, too many teachers have been assigned a book in the absence of a common challenge and have been told it was PLC work.

- **The PLC Planning Time.** Teachers need planning time, no doubt about it. But planning lessons is not what a PLC does. It's planning time. It is true that part of the work accomplished by teachers working collaboratively in professional groups can result in awesome lesson plans, but there is a lot more to an effective meeting of a PLC besides planning lessons.

- **The PLC Data "Admiring" Group.** Data are important fodder for the work that a professional learning community needs to do, but looking at data is not the only work. Too often, teams get bogged down in the data analysis that doesn't go beyond what might be described as observing, remarking, and wondering aloud—in short, admiring the data in all their surprising detail and the complex stories they contain without taking the next step toward action. Sometimes this is because the data admiring takes too long, and other times it's because the team is unaware of the potential they have to use the data to impact learning. Instead, the data analysis often devolves into a discussion about the characteristics of the student body and the seemingly intractable factors that can't be directly influenced by the team, such as poverty. The team remains oblivious to (or perhaps even intimidated by) what they *can* control. Effective PLC groups are action oriented. Data are fuel for the team. They use data to make decisions and then monitor those decisions for their impact on learning.

- **PLC—Survivor Edition.** This one is far too common for many teachers. The team feels it is in survivor mode for a myriad of reasons:

  o They feel an overwhelmed sense of needing to complete limitless forms and documents as well as many other compliance-based tasks. They do not understand why or how they will use these forms and tasks to learn about their students or change their practice.

  o They have the same level of dysfunction as the tribes on the CBS show *Survivor*. There is constant bickering,

> Data are important fodder for the work that a professional learning community needs to do, but looking at data is not the only work.

frustrations are shared, and rarely is anyone thinking about anything except how to fend for themselves and simply *survive*.

- **The PLC PD Meeting.** There are times in all of our lives when we need to learn new things. Those things might be skills or concepts related to teaching and learning. Members attend workshops and conferences, or participate in professional learning opportunities to address a need. That's beneficial, but it's not what PLCs do. PLCs do hard work. PLC members utilize what they have learned to ask hard questions and apply ideas in their classrooms. They dive into data and make decisions that impact learning.

> PLC members utilize what they have learned to ask hard questions and apply ideas in their classrooms.

- **The PLC Meeting.** This is perhaps the most common error of all—a perception that a professional learning community exists only on Wednesday afternoons when teams meet. A PLC is a vibrant and iterative mechanism for engaging in inquiry across space and time. PLCs should operate in the hallways of the school, in the classrooms where we teach, and in the parking lot when we linger to continue a conversation with a colleague. Consider this— you belong to many communities whose membership is defined by shared interests, affiliations, and causes. Your family unit is one such community, and one that exists even when you are not in face-to-face interactions. You don't suddenly become a family when you share a meal together, only to dissolve again when you are apart. A true PLC similarly maintains its shared interests even when its members are apart from one another.

SO WHAT IS A PLC?

The body of literature around PLCs summarizes the two main purposes for them in the preK–12 learning environment:

1. To improve the pedagogical knowledge (skills and knowledge about **how** we teach) and the content knowledge (skills and knowledge about **what** we teach) of educators through collaboration among colleagues

(see Vangrieken, Meredith, Packer, & Kyndt, 2017, for a systematic review of the PLC research).

2. To improve the learning outcomes of students (see Stoll, Bolam, McMahon, Wallace, & Thomas, 2006).

As the work and focus of PLCs has drawn more attention over the decades, we acknowledge that they have also evolved to incorporate an additional purpose, which is to enhance educators' attitudes and dispositions about students and learning. Working toward collective efficacy, taking responsibility for learning, and being flexible in instructional practices transform a PLC from being purely additive to being transformative. Vescio and her colleagues noted that, "although teachers' perceptions about the value of PLCs are both valid and valuable, understanding the outcomes of these endeavors on teaching practice and student learning is crucial, particularly in today's era of scarce resources and accountability" (Vescio, Ross, & Adams, 2008, p. 81). The net effect is that done well, PLCs shift beliefs, mindsets, and behaviors through teacher empowerment. Consider the following questions:

> Working toward collective efficacy, taking responsibility for learning, and being flexible in instructional practices transform a PLC from being purely additive to being transformative.

What is the ultimate goal of your classroom teaching?

Take a moment. Jot your thoughts down. Why do you show up to school every day? When we ask this question of educators, almost to a person, instructional leaders and teachers will use the word *learning*. Although the details will differ, every response will reference some type of *learning*.

If learning is the common thread across responses, how do we ensure that we take steps, each day, to fulfill the goal of learning?

Learning is a process through which experience causes permanent change in thinking or behavior (Woolfolk, Winne, & Perry, 2011). In preK–12 classrooms, instruction is the primary experience. Through instruction, we facilitate students' acquisition of skills and knowledge. As instructional leaders and teachers, we accept the responsibility of teaching students so that they can not only demonstrate mastery of the skills and knowledge contained in our standards and curriculum, but also develop the capacity to be lifelong learners beyond school walls. (By the way, *lifelong learners* is another common phrase used to answer the question about the ultimate goal of schooling.)

We assert that if you want to impact learning, you have to make high-impact decisions about what *and* how to teach. And, if you want to make decisions that have the greatest impact on learning, you have to engage in focused reflection and analysis, or conceptual change, about teaching and learning that will guide you through those decisions. PLCs, when done well, support the thinking, decision making, and learning in our schools and classrooms. They create a space for instructional leaders and teachers to engage in facilitated dialogue around instructional practice, foster innovation, apprentice novice educators, develop pedagogical content knowledge, and make data-informed decisions in our classrooms.

> We assert that if you want to impact learning, you have to make high-impact decisions about what and how to teach.

THE STORY BEHIND PLCs

The history of PLCs goes back 60 years. The need to establish such a collaborative network emerged from the historically isolated nature of teaching and learning. Put differently, we work in a profession where, for many years, it was accepted that "what happens in my classroom is my business and what happens in yours is yours." Closing our classroom doors literally and metaphorically resulted in isolated thinking, decision making, and learning in our schools and classrooms. The result left learning up to chance and required that all educators develop a rich professional knowledge base, refine their own lessons and assessments, and then make isolated decisions about what to do with the results. This also impacted our ability to address gaps in curriculum and instructional decisions being made throughout the school.

In the 1960s, PLCs appeared in the research as a way to offset this isolated approach to teaching and learning. Subsequently, Susan Rosenholtz (1989), in a study of 1,213 teachers from 78 schools, found that learning was enhanced by the collective commitment of teachers in a setting that promoted collaboration. She highlighted this distinction by comparing what she called learning-enriched schools to learning-impoverished schools. Learning-enriched schools promote collaboration, which enhances the commitment of teachers to students and student learning. This idea of collaborative professional networks continues to be a focus in the preK–12 setting.

Simply providing time for professional learning communities to meet is not enough to ensure what Rosenholtz (1989) refers to as a learning-enriched school. Judith Warren Little (1987) reported that teachers benefited from the collaborative work of PLCs when they examined different perspectives, created dissonance, and raised curiosity. However, she noted that simply putting teachers together and telling them to collaborate would not produce the desired outcomes for the teachers. Instead, there must be shared beliefs, values, and norms that promote positive professional relationships among professional learning community members. Furthermore, there must be a culture of collaboration that engages members in reflective practice and inquiry leading to professional growth and supported by mutual support (Little, 1987). Since then, research has continued to explore the role of collaboration through PLCs in schools (e.g., Stoll, Bolam, McMahon, Wallace, & Thomas, 2006), though, as noted above, simply having a PLC does not effectively negate the isolationism common in schools and classrooms. So what are the characteristics of an effective PLC?

Shirley Hord (2004) posed the same question, and sought to develop an evidence-based list of characteristics of effective PLCs. She identified six factors that needed consideration for professional learning communities to thrive:

1. Structural conditions
2. Supportive relational conditions
3. Shared values and vision

COLLABORATIVE WORK WITH YOUR TEAM

Module 1:
Characteristics of an Effective PLC
page 5 in
The PLC+ Playbook

4. Intentional collective learning

5. Peers supporting peers

6. Shared and supportive leadership

In and of themselves, the characteristics are necessary but not sufficient for the implementation of a successful PLC. Thus, the story takes us to the most well-known approach to PLCs—one developed by Richard DuFour, Rebecca DuFour, Robert Eaker, and Thomas Many. This particular model seeks to structure and focus the actual work within the PLC. Moving beyond the six characteristics, this team identified four essential questions designed to drive the conversations of the PLC. These guiding questions put the PLC into action:

1. What is it we want our students to learn?

2. How will we know if each student has learned it?

3. How will we respond when some students do not learn it?

4. How can we extend and enrich the learning for students who have demonstrated proficiency? (DuFour, DuFour, Eaker, & Many, 2010, p. 119)

ADDING THE EXAMINATION OF TEACHING PRACTICE TO THE PLC STORY

The above questions have assisted countless educators in purposefully focusing on student learning, which should rightly be the centerpiece of our mission. Yet there remains a crucial gap in the exclusive examination of student learning, and that is the examination of our *teaching*. Instruction is an essential ingredient that we ignore at our own peril. Imagine a hospital that analyzed only patient outcomes and never queried the medical procedures used. There is a link between learning and teaching, and to examine only one side of the equation limits our ability as educators to take action.

> Yet there remains a crucial gap in the exclusive examination of student learning, and that is the examination of our *teaching*.

There is a reason the fields of medicine and law use the term *practice* to describe what doctors and lawyers do. In both professions, there is a symbiotic relationship between the well-being of the patient/client and the skill of the doctor/lawyer. The practice of medicine is driven by inquiry. *What are the desired outcomes? What worked? What didn't? Why? Were the decisions that led to a treatment plan correct or flawed?*

Likewise, teaching is inquiry. *What are the desired outcomes? What worked? What didn't? Why? Were the decisions that led to a learning plan correct or flawed?* It is necessary to question one's practice, not just outcomes. And we're better when we do this collaboratively rather than individually, because none of us has all of the answers for all of the questions that surface in trying to meet the diverse needs of students. But we also have to develop our own skill set if we are to effectively engage in such inquiry. This is the **plus**.

THE FIVE KEY QUESTIONS

PLC+ provides a framework for the planning and implementation of student learning as well as our own professional learning (e.g., microteaching, classroom observations). Reflected in five essential questions, our **plus** framework asks us to identify:

1. Where are we going?

2. Where are we now?

3. How do we move learning forward?

4. What did we learn today?

5. Who benefited and who did not benefit?

The PLC+ framework, led by the guiding questions above, grounds the work of the PLC in both teaching and learning. As we will see in the subsequent chapters, the use of the pronoun *we* refers to both the learners in our classroom and the learners on our PLC+ team. The **plus** emphasizes not only the learning that we want to occur in students, but also the teaching and learning component for ourselves

PLC+ GUIDING QUESTIONS

1. Where are we going?

This first question is critical. Teams that can answer this question have high levels of teacher clarity. They are keenly aware of the academic standards their students are held accountable to, and they have analyzed these standards to ensure a thorough understanding of the skills, concepts, and rigor level that lie within each standard. That clarity is used to drive the engineering of learning tasks so that evidence of student learning can be gathered and used to make instructional inferences moving forward. This work is often guided by pacing guides and supported with a variety of curricular resources.

2. Where are we now?

In order to answer this question, teams need to have evidence to determine current student proficiency and readiness levels against what they captured in the "Where are we going?" question above. This allows teams to determine appropriate entry points for instruction starting with where students are and moving them to where they need to be. This may require an inventory of existing assessments to identify current resources your team has access to, as well as determining the assessments that will need to be collaboratively designed by the team members. From there, teams identify a common challenge that will drive inquiry into their students' current learning needs.

3. How do we move learning forward?

This question focuses on our teaching practices and the means by which we learn from one another. Learning walks and microteaching are two effective ways to frame the ways in which we analyze our own teaching using the wisdom of peers. These are not the only ways to consider how to best move learning forward. We cross-examine the tasks that we have designed for our students by analyzing assignments for rigor and alignment to standards.

4. What did we learn today?

This is a question often asked of students that has just as much power when asked of the adults. Focusing on this question helps teams to synthesize the information discussed and the data reviewed to examine student progress and achievement. Posing this question to teams helps to ground actions and commitments moving forward. By the same notion, we have to acknowledge the simplicity but significance of this question: *If we gathered and met as a PLC and didn't learn anything, couldn't we have just emailed each other what we talked about?*

COLLABORATIVE WORK WITH YOUR TEAM

**Module 1:
PLC Guiding Questions**
page 8 in
The PLC+ Playbook

as educators. This has been missing from past PLC structures. So, the **plus** in the PLC+ is you. The teacher.

Examining our instruction is now part of the equation.

In the past you, or other teachers working in PLCs, may have felt pressure to have an immediate plan to address or respond to the data put in front of you. In this model, we are acknowledging that the adults present need to reflect on their current practices, determine whether quality experiences have been provided for students, and then continue to learn about practices or strategies that would most likely further impact student learning. We are not just teachers. We are learners, too—lifelong learners—and that needs to be celebrated and encouraged as a necessary part of our profession.

> Examining our instruction is now part of the equation.

WHAT YOU WILL FIND IN THIS BOOK

We have identified and developed four crosscutting and fundamental values that underpin the PLC+ framework. You will find these values discussed and referenced throughout the book, as we explore in depth the work of engaging the five key questions. These four crosscutting values are as follows:

1. **Equity.** The PLC+ needs to be a place where we use information to identify and apply appropriate and impactful evidence-based instructional practices that value the background of every student and help prepare each of them for success. There may be different approaches for different students. In addition to valuing the backgrounds of every student, we must leverage their backgrounds to enhance learning and ensure that the curriculum is responsive and affirming.

2. **High Expectations.** Ensuring we create and maintain high expectations for all students is a critical component of the PLC+ framework. We hold all students accountable to reaching the same bar, yet the pathway by which they arrive at mastery will oftentimes look different. This, of course, is linked to equity.

COLLABORATIVE WORK WITH YOUR TEAM

Module 2:
Crosscutting Values

page 13 in
The PLC+ Playbook

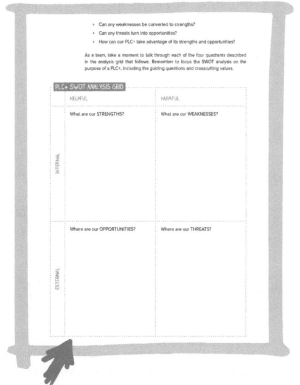

COLLABORATIVE WORK WITH YOUR TEAM

Module 2:
SWOT Analysis

page 16 in
The PLC+ Playbook

3. **Individual and Collective Efficacy.** There is an incredible amount of brain power we can capitalize on when we take our individual capacity and contribute it to a collective whole. This model asks us to build our collective efficacy to create the belief that we can make an impact on each and every one of our students.

4. **Activation.** A high-functioning PLC+ doesn't just happen by chance. The PLC+ needs someone who supports keeping

the discussions focused on its goal and on what members need to do to move forward. This approach requires deliberate efforts as well as structures to ensure these efforts are efficient and focused. It requires **activators**. We don't use the term *facilitator* because, in the truest sense, a facilitator does not contribute to the group but rather focuses on the process. An **activator** not only facilitates the group but also adds ideas, asks questions, notices nonverbal cues, and helps the team make decisions. In other words, the activator is a full member of the team.

> An activator not only facilitates the group but also adds ideas, asks questions, notices nonverbal cues, and helps the team make decisions.

As we move through the PLC+ framework in this book, we will look over the shoulders of a PLC+ team in action as they

- Use the PLC+ questions to maximize student learning in their classrooms as well as their own professional learning. We will take front-row seats as the team unpacks the meaning and intent of each of the five questions and engages in facilitated dialogue around teaching and learning in their classrooms.

- Wrestle with the difficult conversations that come with dialogue around teaching and learning. As each PLC+ team member brings his or her own beliefs, mindsets, and behaviors to the team meeting, how does the team, as a whole, address and respond to potential barriers in the dialogue that could impede the professional learning and student learning in their classrooms?

The PLC+ guiding questions combined with the crosscutting values create a platform that grounds the work of your community, while also considering the lens through which each teacher sees teaching and learning. It will allow you and your team to identify and nurture effective and impactful practices and also provide you with new considerations that have not been in place before. It will provide you with a structure to collaborate and learn. Together, we're better. Together, we're stronger. Together, we achieve more.

We believe that you, the teacher, have been missing from the professional learning community. We don't mean your attendance, or even your cognitive engagement, but rather the fact that the history of the PLC movement has been almost exclusively focused on students and what they were or were not learning. That's not to say that teachers failed to learn how to implement PLCs or how to intervene with students. But keeping student learning at the forefront requires that we also recognize the vital role that you play in the equation of teaching and learning. This means that PLCs must take on two additional challenges: maximizing your individual expertise, and harnessing the power of the collaborative expertise you can develop with your peers.

This imperative is borne out in the research. Byrk, Camburn, and Louis (1999) suggest that the direct impact of PLCs on student learning may not yet be as strong as we would like it to be. For example, schools with PLCs that do not plan, design, and implement rigorous learning experiences will likely see less growth in student learning than schools without PLCs that provide rigorous learning experiences for learners. This is particularly important for schools, classrooms, and teachers seeking to close an achievement gap to acknowledge. So, how do we move forward and narrow the focus even further on the *learning*? We believe that the answer lies in expanding the focus to *teaching*. As we mention above, if we want to change the learning in our school or classroom, we have to change our teaching. If we want to change our teaching, we have to change our decisions and our thinking.

This book is about developing stronger and more effective PLCs, but this challenge is impossible to meet without the next part of

Video 2
Introduction to Chapter 1

resources.corwin.com/
plcplus

13

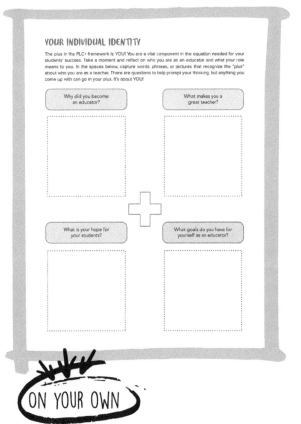

Module 3:
Your Individual
Identity
page 20 in
The PLC+ Playbook

the story—the **plus:** supporting teachers in knowing what to do in the context of individual and collective efficacy, expectations, equity, and the facilitation of learning, both for students and for staff. We hold the following beliefs about the structure and function of teams as they work collaboratively to improve student learning:

1. We must keep the equity of access and opportunity to learn at the forefront of each PLC+ collaborative team meeting.

2. We must ensure that the dialogue provoked by the five questions is facilitated in such a way that the work of the PLC+ is not hindered or impeded.

3. We must develop learning experiences that make our expectations for learning clear to all students.

The collaborative work of the PLC+ should leverage teachers' individual efficacy into collective teacher efficacy. This is done by intentionally extracting the individual expertise each teacher brings to harness and act upon the collective expertise of the group. Honoring these beliefs requires deliberate practice and intentionality. In the following chapters we address how PLCs can address each of the five guiding questions that drive the work:

1. Where are we going?

2. Where are we now?

3. How do we move learning forward?

4. What did we learn today?

5. Who benefited and who did not benefit?

But before we engage in these questions, we need to take a moment and consider the ingredients that make up a strong PLC.

TEACHER CREDIBILITY AND EFFICACY: THE FOUNDATION OF THE STRONG PLC+

We all know that amazing teacher down the hall who continually gets impressive results from students. Some colleagues might say it's because the principal favors that teacher and gives her the highest-performing students. Others say it's because she works all day and night and doesn't have a life outside of school. Still others say that she was "born to be a teacher" and she doesn't have to work that hard at all. But, in our hearts, we know none of those claims are true. We recognize that this particular teacher is talented and has developed a skill set that results in better learning for her students.

There are probably several factors that contributed to this teacher's success, including her credibility and efficacy. We'll explain each of these in the sections that follow. But remember that our focus is on the collective, not solely on the individual. We're exploring these two concepts because we believe that individual teacher credibility and individual teacher efficacy can become **collective** credibility and efficacy when teams of teachers engage in learning together.

> We believe that individual teacher credibility and individual teacher efficacy can become **collective** credibility and efficacy when teams of teachers engage in learning together.

Teacher Credibility

Teacher credibility is the belief held by students that they will learn from this adult because this adult is competent, trustworthy, dynamic, and responsive. It has a strong impact on student learning, with an effect size of 0.90. That's far above the average impact on student learning for all actions and influences, which is 0.40 as measured by Hattie (2012), and should result in a significantly higher rate of learning for students. To put it in perspective, teacher credibility has twice the impact of student motivation on student learning. That's powerful. But the question is, what can you do to enhance your credibility?

Students are perceptive about knowing which teachers can make a difference in their learning and, quite frankly, their lives. We believe that "the dynamic of teacher credibility is **always** at play" (Fisher, Frey, & Hattie, 2016, p. 10). For example, teacher credibility has unique challenges as well as enhanced benefits in the establishment of trust within a classroom community. To be very direct, teacher credibility is a major factor when the learners in the classroom do not look like the teacher that greets them at the door as they enter.

There are four components of teacher credibility outlined in the research: trust, competence, dynamism, and immediacy. We briefly describe these below. We took the time to discuss individual teacher credibility and self-efficacy because they are critical ingredients to the work that a professional learning community needs to do, not to make this a self-help book for current collaborative teams. For detailed suggestions to cultivate each of these components, see Bandura (1997).

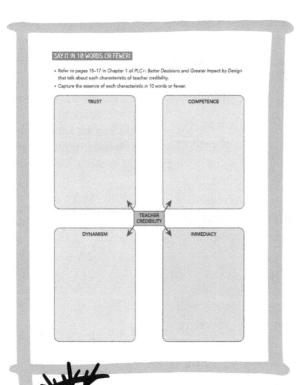

1. **Trust.** Students want to know that their teachers really care about them as individuals and have their best academic and social interests at heart. Students also want to know that their teachers are true to their word and are reliable. Teachers need to come to know their students as people and learners to build relationships. Relational trust is the on-ramp to learning. Students learn best from teachers who they feel care about them.

2. **Competence.** In addition to trust, students want to know that their teachers know their stuff and know how to teach that stuff. They expect an appropriate level of expertise from their teachers in terms of delivery and accuracy of information. A well-paced lesson with accurate information contributes to teacher credibility.

ON YOUR OWN

Module 3:
Teacher Credibility
page 22 in
The PLC+ Playbook

3. **Dynamism.** This aspect of teacher credibility focuses on the passion teachers bring to the classroom and their content. It's really about the ability to communicate your enthusiasm for your subject and your students. And it requires developing dynamic lessons that capture students' interest.

4. **Immediacy.** This final construct of teacher credibility focuses on accessibility and relatability as perceived by students. Teachers need to move around the room and be easy to relate to. Students want to get to know their teachers. Teachers with high credibility make themselves accessible and yet communicate a sense of urgency in the lesson that signals to students that their learning is important.

Before a PLC can develop into the most impactful group possible, it takes everyone on that team to be the best teachers they can be. The PLUS is you, and having credibility with your students isn't a nice-to-have, it's a must!

ON YOUR OWN

Module 3:
Teacher Credibility and Its Intersection With Crosscutting Values
page 23 in
The PLC+ Playbook

Teacher Self-Efficacy

In addition to being credible, we believe that the effective teacher we described at the outset of this section also likely has high self-efficacy. At a basic level, self-efficacy is our individual beliefs that we can reach our goals. It's not self-esteem, which is the worth we place on ourselves. And it's not confidence, as we can be highly confident that we will fail miserably. Instead, as Bandura (1982) noted, self-efficacy is a personal judgment about "how well one can execute courses of action required to deal with prospective situations" (p. 122). People, including teachers, who have high levels of self-efficacy exert sufficient energy to accomplish their goals. In contrast, people (including teachers) who have low self-efficacy tend to give up and do not accomplish their goals. Bandura identified four factors that impact self-efficacy: experiences of mastery, modeling, social persuasion, and physiological contributors.

At a basic level, self-efficacy is our individual beliefs that we can reach our goals. It's not self-esteem, which is the worth we place on ourselves. And it's not confidence, as we can be highly confident that we will fail miserably.

1. **Experiences of Mastery.** The experience of mastery is the single most important factor in developing and reinforcing a person's self-efficacy. When teachers practice together actions and strategies to promote development of mastery, they can determine where their strengths and weaknesses lie. This is one of the most powerful sources of efficacy information (Tschannen-Moran, Woolfolk-Hoy, & Hoy, 1998). When we experience success, or accomplishments, we begin to attribute those successes to our actions rather than outside forces. In other words, success breeds success. We look for situations in which we believe we will be successful, because each success in each such situation reinforces our self-efficacy. Conversely, we tend to avoid situations in which we believe we will fail. Or, if we already have low self-efficacy, we look for confirming evidence that we are not going to be successful.

2. **Modeling.** When we see others succeed, especially when we perceive them to be about the same as ourselves, our self-efficacy increases. To a large extent, people say to themselves, "If they can do it, so can I."

3. **Social Persuasion.** To a lesser extent, encouragement from others builds self-efficacy. We say to a lesser extent because the previous two factors are very powerful. But we don't want to ignore the power of peer support. When we trust the person who encourages us, we can increase our self-efficacy. If the person is honest with us and we believe that that person has our best interests at heart, social persuasion can serve as a tipping point.

4. **Physiological Contributors.** There are a number of physical and biological contributors to our self-efficacy. When we experience stress, our self-efficacy is generally reduced. That is, unless we learn to recognize that stress as part of a natural process. Similarly, when we are frightened, it's hard to maintain self-efficacy. Instead, we move into a flight, fight, or freeze situation. People with higher levels of self-efficacy recognize these physiological factors and understand that they are natural biological responses to situations that do not necessarily signal failure.

TEACHER SELF-EFFICACY

The collective efficacy of a team is derived from the individual efficacy of its members. In turn, the collective efficacy of the team positively influences one's individual sense of efficacy. This doesn't mean that each individual must believe that he or she is an expert about a particular topic. Rather, individual teacher efficacy is fostered by one's sense of self capability. Highly self-efficacious teachers persist, are willing to employ multiple strategies to assist learners, and have warm positive interactions with students. Read pages 17–20 of *PLC+: Better Decisions and Greater Impact by Design* on teacher self-efficacy, and complete the activity below. Capture the essence of each factor by identifying one key word and one key phrase for each one.

EXPERIENCES OF MASTERY	MODELING
SOCIAL PERSUASION	PHYSIOLOGICAL FACTORS

What have you noticed about your own sense of self-efficacy? What experiences have you had that have contributed to your sense of self-efficacy? What experiences have lowered it?

EXPERIENCES THAT BUILD MY SELF EFFICACY	EXPERIENCES THAT LOWER MY SELF EFFICACY
•	•
•	•
•	•

TEACHER SELF-EFFICACY AND ITS INTERSECTION WITH CROSSCUTTING VALUES

The actions we take, the decisions we make, and language of learning we use with students and colleagues reflect the values woven into the fabric of a PLC+. Teacher self-efficacy is influenced by the crosscutting values of equity, high expectations, individual and collective efficacy, and activation.

EVIDENCE WITH STUDENTS	I BUILD MY TEACHER SELF-EFFICACY WHEN I	EVIDENCE WITH COLLEAGUES
	Address equity	
	Establish high expectations	
	Build efficacy	
	Activate learning for myself and others	

ON YOUR OWN

Module 3:
Teacher Self-Efficacy
page 25 in
The PLC+ Playbook

ON YOUR OWN

Module 3:
Teacher Self-Efficacy and Its Intersection With Crosscutting Values
page 26 in
The PLC+ Playbook

The six characteristics of an effective PLC identified by Hord (2004) are built on a strong foundation of credibility and efficacy. Without these two important ingredients, there will be limited capacity for establishing Hord's characteristics: structural conditions, supportive relational conditions, shared values and vision, intentional collective learning, peers supporting peers, and shared and supportive leadership.

But it is a community, not individuals, who need to engage in the work if all students are going to learn at high levels. The answers are in the room. But getting to those answers requires creating systems and supports to unleash potential. In order to move from potential to action, we need to move from the individual to the collective. Together, we are stronger. None of us can individually meet the needs of all of the students in our schools. But together, we can. The PLC+ model is a vehicle for harnessing this strength.

The move to a collective requires, in part, a shared understanding of certain beliefs and norms. This leverages the individual credibility and efficacy of each teacher and is the path toward a collective. It is not "groupthink." There should be room for disagreement and different perspectives about data analysis and action steps, as well as a culture that supports and even promotes dissonance that promotes overall growth. We believe that teams should work to establish their own beliefs and norms. If these beliefs are not present or developed in your current PLC, the *PLC+ Playbook* will support you and your team as they establish beliefs and norms.

FACILITATING COLLABORATION: MAKING THE PLUS COUNT

It is important to note at this point that we believe the collaborative work of professional learning community members should be enabled by people who have developed and practiced their facilitation skills, such as rapport building, communication, listening, questioning the commonplace, and keeping the conversation focused on the goals. We've all been in meetings in which there was no facilitator, or an unskilled one, and we were left feeling frustrated by the experience of having no one to activate the collaborative process. Some of us have this memory fresh in our minds because it has happened recently. In fact, these are the specific experiences and meetings that contribute to our sense that the whole process is pointless and that negatively impact our collective efficacy (Donohoo, 2016). But we hope that the person or persons who facilitate the team also participate in the discussion, so we call them activators rather than facilitators. Elisa MacDonald (2013) identified several hurdles that hinder and even impede what she refers to as a "high-functioning, high-impact, collaborative team" (p. 33). These hurdles include the following:

- One or more of the team members are unable to get along.
- Team members are responsible for meeting the same goals with the same group of students, but they work independently on instruction.

- The team works very well together but has minimal impact on student learning.
- The team lacks leadership, and there is no designated activator to facilitate dialogue.
- The team is focused on tasks—just get it done—but not on professional learning.
- Assessments are viewed with skepticism, and the team focuses on blame and excuses.
- The team meetings are mandated and not wanted by the members.
- There is misalignment between the intentions of the team and their actions.

Our experience shows that individuals or entire collaborative teams may erect hurdles due to issues with teacher credibility, individual efficacy, and collective teacher efficacy. These issues are often rooted in one or more of the crosscutting values that we introduced in the introduction (equity, high expectations, individual and collective efficacy, and activation of groups). For example, a team member may be resistant to changing course in teaching, because he or she is more conditioned to assign blame to certain learners for not benefiting from his or her instruction. Another example might be that a team does not have an individual willing to step up and take the lead, engaging in tough dialogue. For effective facilitation practices for going around, climbing over, or removing each specific barrier, see "15 Barriers and How to Overcome Them" in the *The PLC+ Facilitation and Activator's Guide* by Dave Nagel.

Activators Do Not Need to Be Administrators

All PLC+ teams need to have a strong activator. To be clear, we are not saying that the PLC+ activator must be an administrator. Activators are often teachers who work on the team being facilitated. It's just that the activator needs the skills to lead the group and activate the learning. When there are strong activators, the impact on teachers' teaching and students' learning increases. Without such leadership, "groups may quickly hit a plateau, maintaining a technical focus that prevents them from digging down into and possibly disturbing the assumptions of teaching and learning that maintain the status quo in schools" (Charner-Laird, Ippolito, & Dobbs, 2016, p. 993). For support and guidance on how to be an effective activator, please see *The PLC+ Facilitation and Activator's Guide* by Dave Nagel.

What a Well-Guided PLC Looks Like

As an example of a well-guided and activated group, consider the science team at Hamilton High School. The students at this school hold their science teachers in high regard, often saying things like "There aren't any bad science teachers here" and "They all make sure you really know your science." The team has a reputation for their content knowledge and their skills in meeting individual student needs. In addition, teachers have focused on gathering evidence of impact through growth scores. Both students and teachers take pride in the well-documented learning outcomes of the students' high growth. "Regardless of what you think and know about science, you are going to learn a ton each year," asserts one student. Another student says, "They really want you to learn this stuff, and they can teach it very well. I doubted it before my first unit test. However, the results speak for themselves." In other words, all of the science teachers have strong credibility with students. Their success applies to both growth and achievement in science. For over a decade, they have produced a group of students who compete in regional and state science fairs, winning awards that are proudly displayed in the cabinets in the front of the school.

This PLC+ team doesn't leave their collective success to chance. They have adopted and refined a series of protocols over the last several years to guide their inquiry and investigation. The activator monitors the logistics and the fidelity with which the team is addressing stated goals. In particular, she brokers discussions to ensure that members are heard and understood, and that different perspectives are encourage and examined, and she restates decisions made by the group in order to assist the team in reaching consensus. Importantly, activators of each PLC+ at the school meet regularly to discuss challenges they face, and they support one another in developing solutions.

The science teachers are seen as a collective, and each teacher is very proud of the team's reputation and the ways they work together. The skillful facilitation of the group enhances their work. When new teachers are hired in the department, they are mentored to develop credibility with students. As one of the science teachers said, "We're only as strong as our weakest link. We're not trying to outdo each other. Instead, we build each other up so that we're strong together." You may not work in a high school, or on a science team, but imagine

> This PLC+ team doesn't leave their collective success to chance. They have adopted and refined a series of protocols over the last several years to guide their inquiry and investigation.

the impact of parents saying something like, "I can't wait until my kid is in third grade. That team is amazing. The students love them and they all learn so much about themselves and the world. In fact, they have the highest achievement in the whole school." In both cases, the expectations for success were established early, and the collective teacher credibility served the team well. Importantly, collective credibility reinforces their collective efficacy. And this collective force of credibility has a powerful influence on student learning.

BUILDING COLLECTIVE EFFICACY

Collective efficacy builds on the four areas of self-efficacy that we discussed earlier in this chapter. But the impact is even stronger. Importantly, collective efficacy is the foundation for effective professional learning communities. If a group of teachers goes through the motions of talking about students' learning, but doesn't believe that they have the power to influence that learning, they probably won't have much impact at all. Louis and Kruse (1995) discovered that schools with a genuine sense of community experienced an increased sense of work efficacy, which in turn led to increased classroom motivation and overall satisfaction in their work, and greater collective responsibility for student learning. We believe that teachers need processes and protocols, not to mention facilitation, but they also need to trust in their collective power. They must believe that their students can learn and that they have the power to impact learning. At the collective level, efficacy is built by the following (Bandura, 1986; Donohoo, 2016):

1. **Mastery Experiences.** Like individuals who experience mastery and use that to build self-efficacy, groups that experience success are reinforced for their collective efficacy. As Goddard, Hoy, and Woolfolk Hoy (2004) noted, "Past school successes build teachers' beliefs in the capability of the faculty, whereas failures tend to undermine a sense of collective efficacy" (p. 5). One implication from this aspect of collective efficacy relates to the facilitation of professional learning communities. Activators would be wise to ensure that there are early and regular wins, so that the team begins to see itself as a collective force of nature. In addition, when faced with defeat, the team needs to focus on the parts that were successful, and reengage in efforts to eventually ensure success, not overlooking what they did to reach that success.

A Story of Mastery Experiences

The teachers at Palmdale Elementary School did exactly that. They collaborated to identify gaps in students' literacy learning and developed plans and assessments to close those gaps. They visited each other's classrooms to get ideas for implementation and shared ideas with one another. Over the course of six weeks, they taught and debriefed in grade-level teams. But the benchmark data suggested that English learners and students who lived in poverty did not respond at rates similar to those of other students. The groaning began, and the teachers started to say that their effort did not work. During their next grade-level planning time, the activators, who had met earlier as a group to develop a plan of action, focused on the use of disaggregated data to identify students who had not made expected progress, in order to identify practices that did not work and to develop a specific intervention tailored to those students' needs.

At the next PLC+ meeting, members examined the list of students who had not made expected progress. Taking a case review approach, the group assisted each student's teacher in identifying the child's relative progress, as well as remaining gaps. Systematically, they reviewed each child's strengths, areas of improvement, and cultural background, as well as their current practices used with the student. They then stood back from the data. The activator led the team in categorizing gaps (phonics knowledge, vocabulary, or comprehension) as well as in reflecting on the relevancy of the learning and the ways in which lessons built on students' funds of knowledge. With this increased degree of precision, the team formulated three specific interventions to be utilized with the students who had yet to make progress. "Now let's figure out what our monitoring plan will be, so that we can examine their growth again in six weeks," said one of the team members.

2. **Collective Learning From Models.** Rather than individual teachers experiencing models that impact their efficacy, as was the case with self-efficacy, collective efficacy provides teams of teachers with opportunities to see how others work, or as Bandura called it, "vicarious experiences."

A Story of Learning From Models

The teachers at Mann Middle School decided to visit a school in another district that had similar demographics but much better results with students.

They did not show up to critique the school they were visiting but rather to focus on actions that were different from their own. They saw good instruction but recognized that similar experiences were provided to their students. However, they began to notice that there was instructional consistency across classrooms, rather than isolated examples. As one of the Mann teachers said, "We've seen the same type of note-taking in six different classrooms today." The team engaged in dialogue about the value of consistency in learning strategies and the specific decision by this school to focus on note-taking. "I don't think it's the specific note-taking but the fact that students are given opportunities to practice it over and over," said one team member. They also had a chance to talk with the teachers at the school they visited, asking them several questions. The Mann teachers wanted to know why the other teachers selected specific approaches and how they were able to implement them consistently across the school. This was exactly what the Mann team needed to jump-start their efforts. They discussed a number of instructional routines that differed across the day for students at Mann and committed to implementing some common routines throughout the next several months. This required some members of their team to engage in professional learning around these routines to ensure consistency from classroom to classroom. They also committed to collecting data to determine whether their efforts were impacting student learning, at least in the short term. When the data showed their efforts were effective, the vicarious experience turned into a mastery experience, and their collective efficacy was strengthened.

3. **Social Persuasion.** As we noted earlier, we tend to value people's opinions when we trust them and when we find them credible. Teams do the same. One way to build collective efficacy is through social persuasion. Commonly, this is done by inviting an "expert" to school to share his or her thinking. Outsiders are good for introducing new ideas or serving as a critical friend who is able to say things that insiders cannot say. But our experiences suggest that a valued insider can significantly influence the team as well. And the more cohesive the team is, the more likely they are to be swayed by the comments of the members of their group (Donohoo, 2017). When a member of the team suggests that the team is effective, and provides evidence to support that claim, collective efficacy can increase. Maybe you could be that person for your team.

A Story of Social Persuasion

Carmen Morello was that person on her team who was able to engage her colleagues through social persuasion. The team was talking about a group of black male students who were reportedly "off task" on a regular basis. The conversation this team had focused on culturally relevant learning experiences and the need to engage all students in relevant lessons. As the conversation continued, one of the teachers said, "I'm reflecting on some of our text selections. Really, there are a lot of white females in the books that we commonly use. I think that might be contributing to the issue here. I think we need to revisit our book lists and make sure that students see themselves and others, not just others." At the end of a collaborative team meeting, this typically reserved teacher said, "That was the best conversation I think I've ever had while teaching. We were honest, yet kind. We kept our focus on the needs of students, not the needs of adults. And we developed plans that we all can implement. I'm very impressed by us and I really look forward to working collaboratively again." Of course, professional learning communities are more than meetings; they are a way of life for high-performing schools. But in those schools, teachers have time to meet, and those collaborative teams can build collective efficacy.

> We propose a new type of professional learning community. We're not interested in building a better mousetrap, but rather defining a new way of catching mice.

4. **Affective State**. At the collective level, "the emotional tone of the organization," as Tschannen-Moran and Barr (2004, p. 190) call it, influences the ways in which groups work and how they view their work. These feelings of excitement or stress influence the collective efficacy of the team.

**A Story of Positive PLC+ Influence
on Climate and Culture**

At Hage Elementary School, the climate and culture are palpable. Every visitor comments on the feel of the school and how welcoming it is. The hallways are decorated with student work, including pieces of art, and the classrooms are painted different colors. This specific climate and culture are propagated from the affective state of each PLC+ team. The interactions between team members are positive, and the meetings "feel like a good place to work and learn." In this environment, which is nurtured each day, collective efficacy has a chance of blossoming. Listen for the ways teams talk about themselves.

Identity has been described as the stories we tell ourselves about ourselves. Teams that exist in a high affective state tell stories about their successes, of course, but also about the ways they have overcome struggles.

We hope you have noticed the many ways that an effective professional learning community can mobilize and utilize collective credibility and collective efficacy. It really is a two-way street, with the experiences team members have reinforcing their collective credibility and efficacy and, at the same time, utilizing those resources to ensure successful discussions and actions. In that vein, we have extended the past 60 years' worth of work and propose a new type of professional learning community. In lay terms, we're not interested in building a better mousetrap, but rather defining a new way of catching mice. That's a tall order, given the efforts that have existed to this point. We believe that schools, and the people who work and learn there, are ready to take PLCs to the next level.

THE HOPE FOR THE PLC+

First, it is our hope that the PLC+ model *exemplifies* the collective nature of teachers working together to talk about teaching and learning and then taking action as a result of those discussions. These discussions should center on practices we know strongly impact the growth and achievement of students, as well as the strategies needed to support them, so that we develop a level of automaticity, and these practices eventually become part of every teacher's day-to-day practice. We want to create classrooms and schools where collaboration and collaborative expertise permeate the culture and climate. Second, we hope that the PLC+ framework exposes the *learning* component of the PLC and moves beyond a platform where teachers only share information. Teachers not only need to capitalize on their collective capacity, they also need to afford themselves the opportunity to be learners. And that learning should align directly to the learning needs identified in their students.

There is a moral imperative for a PLC+ to ensure all students—and that means *each* student—are learning and growing. Teams, and

	TEAM MEMBER 1	TEAM MEMBER 2	TEAM MEMBER 3	TEAM MEMBER 4
What information was a surprise for you?				
What was confirmed for you?				
What was the most important thing you learned about yourself?				
What did you discover as being your greatest strength?				
What did you identify as being an area of growth for you?				
How can your teammates encourage and support you in the work of this PLC+?				

FROM INDIVIDUAL TO COLLECTIVE TEACHER EFFICACY

Teams that are empowered to make decisions, act, communicate clearly, and hold themselves accountable for their efforts manifest high degrees of collective teacher efficacy (CTE). Collective teacher efficacy is defined by Goddard and Goddard (2001, p. 809) as "the perceptions of teachers in a school that the faculty as a whole can organize and execute the courses of action required to have a positive effect on students." Importantly, CTE is more than confidence. Read that quote again: "execute the courses of action required." That means seeking evidence of impact on student learning, and responding when the impact is at less than desired levels.

Professional learning communities raise their CTE through foundational commitments to the work (see Donohoo, 2017). Discuss the following PLC+ commitments. In what ways do each of these hold the potential to build CTE? What possible barriers should your team look for that might prevent CTE from growing?

NOTES

_____
_____
_____
_____
_____
_____
_____
_____
_____
_____
_____
_____
_____
_____
_____
_____
_____

COLLABORATIVE WORK WITH YOUR TEAM

Module 4:
Collective Efficacy and Credibility in a PLC+
page 30 in
The PLC+ Playbook

Module 4:
From Individual to Collective Teacher Efficacy
page 33 in
The PLC+ Playbook

Module 4:
Norms for Our Ways of Work in Our PLC+
page 37 in
The PLC+ Playbook

NORMS FOR OUR WAYS OF WORK IN OUR PLC+

MEMBERS	DATE

NORMS

-
-
-
-
-

individual teachers, must have expectations for all students that are high and rigorous. Equity demands that we recognize all learners and the contributions they bring to the classroom, and that they are guaranteed the opportunity to learn in an environment that is safe and accessible, builds on their current funds of knowledge, and embraces the diversity within the classroom. Whether the diversity in a classroom is based on race, readiness levels, socioeconomic status, or other factors, none of these can be used as a barrier to separate the classroom community or the learners who are in the classroom. Thus, last, we hope that this framework creates an embracement of mutual dialogue and respect for all of the learners served, one where implicit biases are identified and discussed and can transform our thinking and behavior so we become critically conscious and culturally competent. When we accomplish these things, our ability to impact the educational trajectories of our students—and even their life trajectories—will be limitless. **This focus on teaching is also a *plus*.** But the plus is you.

CONCLUSION

The PLC+ model aims to contribute to the knowledge base that teams have as they strive to move students forward in their learning. In the five chapters that follow, we explore each of the core questions. In the final chapter of this book, we introduce the idea that a student-centered PLC+, using the same core questions, could become the norm in classrooms led by teachers who have internalized these ideas.

PLC+ features five questions and four crosscutting values that permeate the work: a focus on equity, facilitation to move from discussion to action, high expectations for all students, and a commitment to building individual self-efficacy and the collective efficacy of your professional learning community.

QUESTION 1:

WHERE
Are We
GOING?

PLC+ Framework Guiding Questions

1. **Where are we going?**
2. **Where are we now?**
3. **How do we move learning forward?**
4. **What did we learn today?**
5. **Who benefited and who did not benefit?**

THE STORY BEHIND THE QUESTION

The question "Where are we going?" is the launching point for every PLC+. This question focuses attention on the *intentions* for learning. It challenges us to move beyond pacing guides and curriculum maps to make clear-eyed decisions about the learning path we will blaze. Keep the end in mind: *What is it that we want our learners to know, understand, and be able to do?* This, of course, is not limited to content learning, and can include language development and social and emotional learning outcomes. As PLC+ teams engage in this first question, they will clearly define the learning intentions, success criteria, and learning progressions (or as our colleagues in Canada say, curriculum expectations) that are rooted in the standards for learning established by their state or province, district, and school.

Video 3
Introduction to Chapter 2

resources.corwin.com/
plcplus

The four crosscutting values are interwoven throughout this inquiry. The first crosscutting value is effective **activation** of the discussion and action necessary. This first question requires that the team have the documents, templates, and space to analyze the standards/curriculum and engage in dialogue about the intended learning, the criteria for success, and the sequence of this learning. This is not an intellectual exercise—it builds a solid foundation for what is to follow. **Equity** is embedded in the team's work through establishing a clear understanding of what *all* students need to learn. All students the PLC+ serves need to learn at high levels, not by chance but by design. If teachers are unclear about what their students should be learning and how it will be measured, there is lessened chance their students will be able to learn. Close examination of grade-level standards, no matter how frequently they have been taught in the past, ensures **expectations** are appropriately recalibrated among team members consistently. Next, and of critical importance, the rigor level of the standard/curriculum should remain the constant, while the pathway for how students arrive at mastery of the standard/curriculum might look different. Taking the time to analyze standards/curriculum expectations in order to look at the skills and concepts within them drives the design of learning intentions and success criteria for students. These represent nonnegotiable components of learning for all students and ensure appropriate expectations are set for every learner.

The rigor level of the standard/curriculum should remain the constant, while the pathway for how students arrive at mastery of the standard/curriculum might look different.

When teams establish a consistent practice of reviewing standards/curriculum expectations, pacing guides, and resources, this helps the PLC+ to develop strong collaborative armor and to learn and grow from each other. You will recall that **individual and collective efficacy** stems from perceptions of teachers that the team "can organize and execute the courses of action required to have a positive effect on students" (Goddard & Goddard, 2001, p. 809). Working collaboratively with a focus on these values provides opportunities for your team to tap into the collective expertise and determine ways in which all students will achieve at high levels.

Finally, we offer a reminder about the ultimate purpose of a professional learning community. The unswerving focus is on promoting students' learning through careful analysis of their progress. While Module 6 in *The PLC+ Playbook* features some of the planning elements described in this chapter, it is not our intention to turn a PLC+ into a forum for lesson planning. We assume that teachers spend time planning with one another, or individually, at other times. The initial focus on analyzing the standards is so that teams can come to agreement on what will be taught and measured. But this is only one-fifth of the inquiry cycle in the PLC+ framework. As we have noted previously, "Begin with the end in mind." In this case, the end point is analysis and response to student learning, not lesson design.

A PLC+ TEAM IN ACTION

Kathy Garber and her other PLC+ members have been meeting on Wednesdays for the entire semester. This group of high school English 9 teachers systematically reviews students' progress on their current units of study and engages in thinking, decision making, and learning about the upcoming unit. "Our PLC+ team meetings are part of a continual process. We are never finished. As a team, we circle back around and use the five essential questions as an iterative process for our ongoing learning and embedded professional development. Sometimes, we focus on a question in more depth, as we will do today when we analyze standards for an upcoming unit. Other times we focus on students' learning and how we might make changes to increase their learning," Ms. Garber says.

Ms. Garber will activate the dialogue for today's collaborative team meeting, but other days other colleagues serve as the activator. This division of labor allows each of the members to facilitate the aspect of their learning community that is most comfortable for them, while at the same time making sure that a single individual does not dominate the conversation. In other schools, the activator remains constant over months or the entire school year.

Today, Ms. Garber and her colleagues engage in the question "Where are we going?" given that next week is the start of the fourth quarter. As part of their discussion, they conduct a deliberate, intentional, and purposeful examination of the English content standards, the district pacing guides, and the other associated curriculum documents provided by both the district office and state department of education. These documents include the template for analyzing standards, planning template, test blueprints, and released test items.

Analyzing standards/curriculum expectations is an important step in ensuring equity for students. In order to have equity, teachers have to have high expectations for all students. To do this they need to first know and understand their grade-level standards/expectations and what these expectations ask students to be able to know and perform. After all, an amazing lesson for fifth graders on third-grade standards will produce sixth graders who are ready for fourth grade. It just exacerbates the inequities that some students experience.

> After all, an amazing lesson for fifth graders on third-grade standards will produce sixth graders who are ready for fourth grade. It just exacerbates the inequities that some students experience.

Ms. Garber starts the meeting by referencing the district pacing guide for the third nine-week period of the school year. In talking about her collaborative team meetings, she states that "revisiting the standards is something we do to recalibrate. We had noticed as a team that after the standards were introduced, we spent lots of time working with them. But after a few years we got comfortable and complacent." She continues, "That's when we saw from examining our data that there had been some slippage. We just weren't expecting as much as we used to from our students." The standards the PLC+ reviewed are shown in Figure 2.1.

The focus of the first part of the third quarter draws from the Common Core State Standards for ninth- and tenth-grade English (National Governors Association Center for Best Practices & Council of Chief State School Officers, 2010). "The alignment between our district's pacing guide and the specific content and process standards is vital in ensuring that we are going in the correct direction and to the correct learning intention and success criteria," Ms. Garber comments.

English Language Arts Standards » Reading: Literature » Grades 9–10

CCSS.ELA-LITERACY.RL.9-10.4

Determine the meaning of words and phrases as they are used in the text, including figurative and connotative meanings; analyze the cumulative impact of specific word choices on meaning and tone (e.g., how the language evokes a sense of time and place; how it sets a formal or informal tone).

Source: © Copyright 2010. National Governors Association Center for Best Practices and Council of Chief State School Officers. All rights reserved.

FIGURE 2.1   **Pacing Guide for the Third Nine Weeks**

Reading Literature

Key Ideas and Details

RL.9.1   Cite strong and thorough textual evidence to support analysis of what the text says explicitly as well as inferences drawn from the text.

RL.9.2   Determine the theme(s) or central idea(s) of a text and analyze in detail the development over the course of the text, including how details of a text interact and build on one another to shape and refine the theme(s) or central idea(s); provide an accurate summary of the text based upon this analysis.

Craft and Structure

RL.9.4   Determine the meaning of words and phrases as they are used in the text, including figurative and connotative meanings; analyze the cumulative impact of specific word choices on meaning and tone (e.g., how the language evokes a sense of time and place; how it sets a formal or informal tone).

Integration of Knowledge and Skills

Range of Reading and Level of Text Complexity

RL.9.10   By the end of Grade 9, read and comprehend literature, including stories, dramas, and poems, in the grades 9-10 text complexity band proficiently, with scaffolding as needed at the high end of the range.

Now her team begins the process of analyzing the standards/ expectations to develop a clear understanding of what students are expected to know, understand, and be able to do. This provides a clear path forward by allowing classroom teachers to see what students *need* to know, understand, and be able to do while at the same time providing teachers the opportunity to make conscious decisions to stay the course and to avoid the distractions and digressions of what is just *neat* to know, understand, and be able to do.

ANALYZING THE STANDARD(S)/CURRICULUM EXPECTATIONS

Below are the steps to analyzing a standard/curriculum expectation to answer the question "Where are we going?"

Select the specific standard(s) for the specific content aligned with the pacing guide.

In this specific scenario, Ms. Garber and her colleagues use CCSS .ELA-LITERACY.RL.9-10.4 based on the pacing guide that has been provided by her district. Some districts do not have pacing guides, and teams of teachers must identify times during the year when standards are taught and assessed.

Discuss the content of the standard and identify concepts (nouns).

Ms. Garber and her colleagues first look at the nouns and noun phrases that represent the ideas, concepts, or topics students must know and understand. Nouns are vocabulary, ideas, concepts, and topics within the standard. Ms. Garber and her colleagues move through CCSS .ELA-LITERACY.RL.9-10.4 line by line to underline the nouns within the standard. This section of the standards is shown in Figure 2.2.

FIGURE 2.2 Underlined Nouns Within the Standard

CCSS.ELA-LITERACY.RL.9-10.4

Determine the meaning of words and phrases as they are used in the text, including figurative and connotative meanings; analyze the cumulative impact of specific word choices on meaning and tone (e.g., how the language evokes a sense of time and place; how it sets a formal or informal tone).

Not all nouns deserve the same attention. For example, one of Ms. Garber's colleagues feels strongly that the term *cumulative impact* must be emphasized so that learners can build their conceptual understanding of how word choice impacts an entire text. He asserts,

"I really think we have to help them see this [cumulative impact] conceptually so they don't just understand the meanings of words and phrases in isolation."

Another member of the team adds, "I think we've really only focused on words, but the standard says *words and phrases*. I looked at the released test items, and there are several that are phrases and not just words. We'll need to change that this year and place more emphasis on specific, targeted vocabulary. We need to think about how phrases impact the text and how those are understood by our students."

Identify the skills (or verbs) in the standard/expectations.

As the team agrees on the ideas, concepts, or topics, they move to the verbs. Verbs represent the depth at which their learners must engage with these ideas, concepts, or topics. Essentially, this is what the learners must do with the content and process or the knowledge and understandings. To ensure that Ms. Garber and her colleagues have a clear picture of these performance expectations, they circle the relevant verbs within the standard. This language is shown in Figure 2.3.

FIGURE 2.3   Circled Verbs Within the Standard

CCSS.ELA-LITERACY.RL.9-10.4

(Determine) the meaning of words and phrases as they are used in the text, including figurative and connotative meanings; (analyze) the cumulative impact of specific word choices on meaning and tone (e.g., how the language evokes a sense of time and place; how it sets a formal or informal tone).

Source: © Copyright 2010. National Governors Association Center for Best Practices and Council of Chief State School Officers. All rights reserved.

A third colleague in the room speaks up and says, "We need to ensure that learners have a strong understanding of what it means to do an analysis so that they are able to synthesize the different meanings in a text as a whole. The verb *analyze* requires a number of subskills the student will need to apply. To analyze the impact of words, phrases, and meanings to determine the cumulative impact on meaning and tone, you have to be able to dissect what each of those mean on their own and the role they play within the text before being able to put them all together to support an analysis."

ANALYZING STANDARDS

1. What are the concepts (nouns/noun phrases) in the standard? Underline the concepts in the standard.
2. What are the skills (verbs) in the standard? Circle the verbs in the standard.

ANALYSIS TEMPLATE EXAMPLE FOR THIRD GRADE

ELA-Literacy RI.3.2: Determine the main idea of a text, recount the key details and explain how they support the main idea.

CONCEPTS (NOUNS AND NOUN PHRASES)	SKILLS (VERBS)
Main idea of a text	Determine
Key details	Recount
How key details support main idea	Explain

COLLABORATIVE WORK WITH YOUR TEAM

Module 5:
Analyzing Standards
page 40 in
The PLC+ Playbook

In response, another teacher says, "I'm not sure that I even understand what this means. I'm not sure how students can analyze this in this way. I guess I'm thinking of the tasks that we will assign, and I know that we're not there yet, but learning to analyze for a cumulative impact is really hard. But the analysis is supposed to be focused on two things, right? It's about both meaning and tone. That means we really need to develop lessons that have students analyze the meanings of the texts and lessons on analyzing the tone."

Develop a learning progression leading to what students are expected to know, understand, and be able to do.

Now that the team has devoted significant time to discussing the concepts and the skills (nouns and the verbs) of the standard/expectation, they have uncovered some skills and processes that need careful instructional planning (i.e., synthesis of word choice on meaning and tone). Now they turn their attention to the development of a learning progression leading to what students are expected to know, understand, and be able to do. This is the core of where we are going in terms of students' learning.

Determining a learning progression is twofold. It requires the team to think about the subskills or enabling knowledge required to access and master the skills and concepts within the standard as a whole. In this sense, it aligns with Popham's (2008) definition of a learning progression as a carefully sequenced set of building blocks that students must master en route to mastering a more distant curricular aim. These building blocks consist of subskills and bodies of enabling knowledge. It also requires the team to take the underlined nouns and associated verbs and arrange them in a way that the team believes represents a logical progression for learning these ideas, concepts, or topics. This of course relies on research in teaching and learning, as well as on professional judgment and on how the team believes it is best to approach this particular standard/expectation.

It is important to remember, however, that learning isn't linear, and while teachers need to determine the sequence of instruction as they best see it, students may learn it in a different order.

There are a number of questions that teams can use to think about an appropriate progression of learning for students. There is no one, right way to organize the flow of learning, but there are probably incorrect ways. Some of the questions that we have found useful in leading discussions about learning intentions include the following:

- What prior knowledge is necessary for learners to successfully engage in this learning?

- What skills and concepts did students need to master in prior standards?

- What learning experiences must they have to successfully build their prior learning and background knowledge?

- What key vocabulary is explicit or implicit within the verbiage of the standard or curriculum expectations.

- What scaffolding is necessary for all learners to successfully engage in this learning?

- What do we know about students that can make these learning experiences more meaningful?

Ms. Garber's team spent about 10 minutes identifying the range of subskills and required knowledge that students would need to successfully demonstrate mastery of the standard. They then placed them in a sequence that they believed could best accelerate students' learning. Their list has 31 different topics (Figure 2.4). Importantly, that does not mean that they will *spend 31 days on this standard* but rather that there are 31 learning steps that they need to address and check

COLLABORATIVE WORK WITH YOUR TEAM

Module 5:
Design the
Learning Progression
page 42 in
The PLC+ Playbook

FIGURE 2.4   Brainstorming the Learning Progression

Sample Learning Progression for Standard RL 9-10.4: Determine the meaning of words and phrases as they are used in the text, including figurative and connotative meanings; analyze the cumulative impact of specific word choices on meaning and tone (e.g., how the language evokes a sense of time and place; how it sets a formal or informal tone).

1. **Define** *determine.*

2. **Define** *context clue.*

3. **Determine** different types of context clues.

4. **Identify** unknown words in a sentence.

5. **Identify** context clues present in a sentence that support word meaning.

6. **Recognize** types of context clue(s) present that support word meaning.

7. **Explain** how context clues support determining the meaning of the unknown word.

8. **Determine** the meaning of the unknown word in the sentence.

9. **Identify** unknown words in a paragraph.

10. **Identify** context clues present in a paragraph that support word meaning.

11. **Recognize** types of context clue(s) present that support word meaning.

12. **Explain** how context clues in the paragraph support determining the meaning of the unknown word(s).

13. **Determine** the meaning of unknown words in a paragraph.

14. **Identify** unknown words in a text.

15. **Identify** context clues present in the text that support word meaning.

16. **Recognize** types of context clue(s) present that support word meaning.

17. **Explain** how context clues in the text support determining the meaning of the unknown word(s).

18. **Determine** the meaning of the unknown word(s) in a text.

19. **Define** *figurative language.*

20. **Recognize** different types of figurative language.

21. **Identify** figurative language in a sentence or paragraph.

22. **Determine** the meaning of the figurative language identified.

23. **Define** *tone.*

24. **Define** *connotation.*

25. **Define** *denotation.*

26. **Identify** words with positive connotations.

27. **Identify** words with negative connotations.

28. **Determine** the connotative meaning of the identified words.

29. **Explain** how the identified words impact the tone of the text.

30. **Analyze** the cumulative impact of word choice on tone.

31. **Analyze** the cumulative impact of word choice on meaning.

for understanding along the way. Many of these can be addressed in a few minutes and quite often are prerequisite understanding most students already possess. Others will require more instructional time. A list of learning progressions carefully crafted provides a diagnostic roadmap for teachers to use to determine where the learning gaps exist when students struggle with a larger curriculum aim. Eventually, the team will transform the learning progressions into learning intentions, or the daily expectations for learning.

To ensure that teachers are creating an inclusive learning environment that provides equity for each learner, teams must establish consistent expectations for each student. By focusing on the skills and concepts in the standard, we ensure that all students are held to the true expectations expressed in the standard/curriculum. This point cannot be overstated—learning in our schools and classrooms is a civil right, available to each and every student that passes through the doorway. Safeguarding this right begins with establishing clear expectations that are not dependent on learners' demographic or background characteristics. Furthermore, this significant part of the process drives the development of the learning progression as well as every subsequent decision about the learning experience. For the standard Ms. Garber's team was working with, students may engage at different locations of the learning progression or need additional support to demonstrate proficiency or mastery of this standard. This understanding of the learning progression for the standard also provides the team with insight into areas that need to be explored and addressed in subsequent meetings. Developing learning progressions collaboratively periodically throughout the school year also is an action that supports the PLC+ team in developing collective efficacy through positive interdependence.

In summary, analyzing standards provides a clear path forward by allowing classroom teachers to see what students *need* to know, understand, and be able to do while at the same time providing us the opportunity to make conscious decisions, based on evidence of student learning, to stay the course and avoid drift.

THE ROLE OF TEACHER CLARITY IN "WHERE ARE WE GOING?"

To achieve what they want in the classroom, teachers need clarity—a deep understanding about what to teach and why, how to teach it, and what success looks like. This goes beyond simply being familiar with the day's lesson. Moreover, it involves an ongoing process that enables teachers both to understand deeply themselves what is to be learned and to communicate those same aspects to their students in student-friendly language. There are two parts to teacher clarity that are especially relevant to this first question. The first is being clear about what is to be learned from the lesson, variously called the learning intention, objective, or target. (For the sake of consistency, we will refer to it as the learning intention.) A second dimension of teacher clarity is apparent when students and the teacher have a shared understanding of the evidence to show the desired learning has been achieved, also called the success criteria.

It is the teacher's ability to communicate learning intentions and success criteria that ensures that learning is transparent for students, and this is an important contributor to teacher credibility.

The work involved in analyzing standards and developing learning intentions and success criteria is a worthwhile investment, as teacher clarity has a strong effect size of 0.75 (Hattie, 2012). But keep in mind that simply plastering the walls with laminated versions of both will not result in accelerated student learning. Breakthrough results only occur when these are coupled with instruction and assessment that are tightly aligned to them. Teachers must communicate these to the students and make the learning transparent. This transparency is an important contributor to teacher credibility. Making sure students are aware of the learning destination as well as the pathway for success ensures equity in access to the learning for students. In addition, when teacher clarity is present as part of a PLC+ structure, there is a greater assurance that universal expectations for learning are in place for all students, and while the readiness levels of learners may vary, the expectations for success do not.

DEVELOPING LEARNING INTENTIONS AND SUCCESS CRITERIA

To maximize the impact on student learning, it is not enough for Ms. Garber and her colleagues to know where they are going in English 9 during the first part of the fourth quarter of the school year. They—and all of us—must articulate to students where the learning is headed every day. In fact, there is evidence that students who know what they are learning are more likely to actually learn it (Wiliam, 2011). The English 9 PLC+ will utilize their analysis of the standard to create daily learning intentions and success criteria for helping students master the standard/expectation as a whole.

As Ms. Garber's team now turns its attention to making the learning visible to the students, they develop the learning intentions and success criteria for learning in three areas: content, language, and social intentions. Dividing learning intentions into *content, language,* and *social* purposes can provide teachers and students alike a clearer sense of each day's expectations.

> *Content learning intentions* answer the question "What is the content that I am supposed to use and learn today?"

> *Content learning intentions* articulate what it is that students are learning and relate directly to the essential skills, knowledge, and understandings presented in the standards.

> *Language learning intentions* answer the question "How should I communicate my thinking today?"

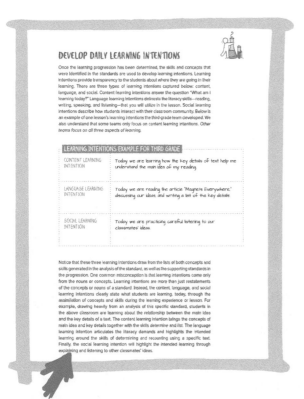

COLLABORATIVE WORK WITH YOUR TEAM

Module 5:
Develop Daily
Learning Intentions

page 45 in
The PLC+ Playbook

Language learning intentions provide a venue for us to lay out the language demands of the day: Are students developing new academic or content vocabulary? Are they practicing recently developed vocabulary within proper linguistic structures, or are they using those structures for communicative functions (e.g., to explain, to speculate, to express an opinion)? This is not limited to verbal communication and can include written or verbal representations of thinking across all content areas. This aspect of the learning intention focuses on how students will use language to access content and demonstrate understanding of that content. The language learning intention is typically very useful in developing the success criteria (which are explained below).

Social learning intentions answer the question "How should I interact with my classroom community today?"

Social learning intentions allow teachers to develop and leverage social or social-emotional learning outcomes within their classroom culture.

Ms. Garber's team communicates daily learning intentions to their students through these content, language, and social lenses, as they find it gives them the flexibility to target different areas of growth for different students. They also suggest that this dynamic approach helps ensure they are addressing the bigger picture of learning—like how we communicate and compare our thinking to that of others so we can grow further. For example, on the first day of this unit, the team plans on the following learning intentions:

- *Content learning intention:* We are learning about how authors use word choice in dialogue as a means for indirect characterization.

- *Language learning intention:* We will be explaining this technique using evidence from the text in discussion with peers.

- *Social learning intention*: We are asking clarifying questions of one another to understand ideas.

Each of the English 9 teachers on Ms. Garber's team begins the day by reviewing the learning intentions, briefly discussing them, and then using them periodically throughout the lesson to keep students focused and progressing in their learning. Teachers know where they are going, and so do the learners. The members of the team do not simply use the content standard/curriculum expectation as the sole learning intention. Instead, they believe in the process discussed above and the adaption of the unpacked standard/expectation into learning intentions written in student-friendly language. They have identified chunks that can be learned in a given day. Standards are large and need to be broken into component parts so that students (and teachers) know what students need to learn each day.

Notice that the three learning intentions developed by Ms. Garber's team draw from the list of both concepts and skills generated in the analysis of the standard, as well as the supporting standards in the progression. Ms. Garber points out that "early on we believed that learning intentions come only from the nouns in the standard." Learning intentions are more than just restatements of the concepts or nouns of a standard. Instead, the content, language, and social learning intentions clearly state what students are learning, today, through the assimilation of concepts and skills during the learning experience or lesson. For example, drawing heavily from our clear understanding of this specific standard, students are learning about the relationship between the author's use of word choice and indirect characterization. The content learning intention brings the concepts of word choice and indirect characterization together with the use of these concepts in writing. The language learning intention articulates the literacy demands and highlights the intended learning around the skills of explaining and using specific evidence from the text. Finally, the social learning intention highlights the intended learning through explaining and listening to other classmates' ideas through clarifying questions.

> Dividing learning intentions into *content*, *language*, and *social* purposes can provide teachers and students alike a clearer sense of each day's expectations.

Ms. Garber emphasizes that through activating dialogue within her team, they came to understand that learning intentions

- Articulate what learners are expected to learn during today's learning experience

- Help learners see why they are learning this particular content and these skills

- Should not be restatements of the standards

- Should not focus solely on the concepts or nouns in the standard

Success criteria are directly linked with learning intentions. The team develops the success criteria for each learning intention. There needs to be at least one success criterion for each learning intention, but there can be several success criteria for each learning intention. Success criteria are developed by the teacher and/or the students and describe what success looks like. They help the teacher and student to make judgments about the quality of student learning. Ms. Garber's team uses "I can" statements to craft their success criteria. For example, they created the following success criteria for the learning intentions described above:

- I can explain how word choice in dialogue influences the tone of a text.

- I can determine the meaning of an unknown word using contextual analysis.

Just as learning intentions do not solely focus on the concepts or nouns, success criteria are more than verbs. Ms. Garber and her team think of success criteria as the evidence learners are expected to produce that will make their learning progress visible. How can learners make their learning visible? From the teacher's perspective, what will learners do that will indicate that they are making progress in their learning or where they need additional learning? For example, what will the learners in the above classroom be expected to do to make their learning visible around word choice in dialogue and the tone of the text? Ms. Garber and her team will be looking for this evidence during the learning experience or lesson.

Such success criteria point students to the level of learning expectation and allow students to set goals for their own learning. They also allow students to monitor their own progress and determine when they have achieved success.

For more about writing successful learning intentions and success criteria, see *The Teacher Clarity Playbook* (Fisher, Frey, Amador, & Assof, 2018) and *Clarity for Learning* (Almarode & Vandas, 2018).

IT'S NOT JUST HIGH SCHOOL ENGLISH

We have profiled a ninth-grade English language arts standard as an example of the process. But it works for any grade or content area. For example, the teachers at Vista Del Monte Elementary School analyzed the standards in science, and, after considering data generated by formative and summative assessments and identifying the need to enhance writing in content areas, they decided to add a focus on writing schoolwide. When grade-level teams met, they followed the same process as Ms. Garber and her colleagues used for determining where they were going. In addition to analyzing the standards/expectations, developing learning progressions, and creating learning intentions and success criteria for science, they also decided to incorporate writing outcomes into each of the content areas. For example, one of the learning intentions for third-grade science is to learn ways to defend scientific inferences, so the team added an associated success criterion: *Learners demonstrate that they can develop an argumentative essay to defend their assertions about an animal's survival in a specific habitat.* In kindergarten, students were learning to write a descriptive sentence about a character in a story, while fifth graders were asked to engage in narrative writing as they developed a fictional story that utilized mean, median, and mode.

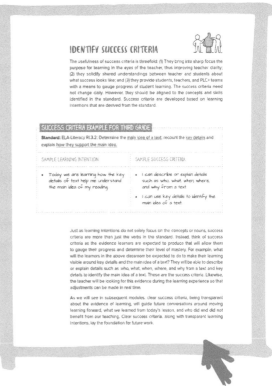

COLLABORATIVE WORK WITH YOUR TEAM

Module 5:
Identify Success Criteria
page 48 in
The PLC+ Playbook

Let's take a look at the work of a few more teams to get a sense of how various groups of teachers have analyzed standards to answer the first PLC+ question: "Where are we going?" For example, a fifth-grade team focused on mathematics identified the following:

Standard:

CCSS.MATH.CONTENT.5.OA.A.2

(Write) simple expressions that record calculations with numbers, and (interpret) numerical expressions without evaluating them.

Source: © Copyright 2010. National Governors Association Center for Best Practices and Council of Chief State School Officers. All rights reserved.

Standard Unpacked:

CONCEPTS (Nouns and noun phrases)	SKILLS (Verbs)
Simple expressions that record calculations without numbers	Write
Numerical expressions without evaluating them	Interpret

The learning intentions they developed include the following:

Content Learning Intention	We are learning how to write expressions from the given information.
Language Learning Intention	We are learning to explain why our expressions contain all of the information given.
Social Learning Intention	We are learning to take turns in sharing our interpretations.

The success criteria they identified included these:

- I can interpret numerical expressions.
- I can write an expression with all of the given information.

Of course, there would be many more learning intentions and success criteria for this standard that would progress over many days. Sometimes, instructional materials provide a pace or scope with learning intentions. In those cases, teams can check to see whether they agree with the flow of the lessons and whether they believe that the standard has been analyzed and presented in a way that students can master the content. In other cases, the materials do not provide learning intentions and success criteria, and teams need to use the instructional materials having analyzed the standards and sequenced the lessons themselves.

MOVING BEYOND A SINGLE DAY

As we continue to follow the work of the PLC+ collaborative team meeting between Ms. Garber and her colleagues, keep in mind that we are witnessing them develop the initial learning intentions and success criteria for this unit. Over the course of their collaborative and individual work, they will continue to develop daily learning intentions and success criteria. However, the effectiveness of creating these expectations will depend on where their learners are and how they move forward in the learning. For example, mapping out daily learning intentions and success criteria for the entire unit may prove to be ineffective and inefficient. What if learners do not progress at a pace that aligns with these predetermined learning intentions and success criteria? What if Ms. Garber's team learns that students are missing important background knowledge and prior knowledge? Having a shared understanding of and clarity about learning progressions for their students is one thing. Effectively using collaboration time, initial assessment data, and formative assessment data to make the next instructional decision, including the next day's learning intentions and success criteria, is another. This PLC+ team has a clear starting point and a learning progression to guide their thinking. However, they will be responsive to where their learners are in planning days 2, 3, 4, and so on. They are now able to intentionally and decisively respond to

COLLABORATIVE WORK WITH YOUR TEAM

Module 5:
Complete PLC+ Template for Guiding Question 1: Where Are We Going?
page 50 in
The PLC+ Playbook

students' needs, because they took the time to craft a set of learning progressions that provide them a way to monitor the ongoing progress of their students formatively, rather than wait until the end of a unit and conduct an autopsy.

AUTONOMY IN TEACHING

As Ms. Garber brings this PLC+ team meeting to a close, they are clear in their answer to the question "Where are we going?" Ms. Garber knows this because the team has developed significant trust with one another. At this meeting, Ms. Garber asks her colleagues to vote "fist to five" in response to the question about their comfort with the standard and the learning progression they developed. A closed fist means totally uncomfortable, and then it scales from one to five, with five being highly comfortable. All of the teachers indicate a four or a five, suggesting that they have a clear understanding of the following:

1. The standard/expectation associated with the pacing guide and curriculum documents provided by their district

2. The specific content and skills of learning expected by the standard/curriculum expectation

3. The progression of learning that will lead to learners developing proficiency or mastery of the standard/expectation

4. The first set of learning intentions and success criteria in student-friendly language

During the few remaining minutes of the PLC+ meeting, one of Ms. Garber's colleagues, a first-year teacher, asks, "So do we all have to be doing the same lesson on the same day? I am comfortable with the standard, now that we have analyzed it, and I really like the progression of learning. That would have taken me hours and hours to do on my own. But I'm worried that I am supposed to be at the exact same place as everyone else in the unit."

This question is common within grade levels, departments, and across schools and districts. Pacing guides combined with common planning for a PLC+ team are often misinterpreted as a mandate that all teachers must be on page 42 of the textbook by the same date, must offer the same assignments or tasks, or must provide the exact same homework or practice tasks as their colleagues. As far as we are concerned, this is a misconception and not the vision, mission, or goal of PLC+. Although we recognize that some districts and schools do adopt this approach, research on scripted or programmed instruction indicates that the rate of learning is far less than average, with an effect size of 0.23. Instead, we argue that a better goal is for all members of the PLC+ to be in agreement about where they are going in the learning, as well as how they will determine collectively how their students are progressing—a topic we will address in Chapter 3. These are nonnegotiable. How various teachers get there is part of the art and science of teaching. Having said that, we think another mistake of some PLC models is the lack of attention to high-quality, evidence-based instruction. We believe teams of teachers should talk about their ideas for effective learning experiences for students. Each teacher should not have to rediscover every instructional strategy or create every task for students. Sharing is the name of the game. Thus, our answer to questions about being at the same place on the same day as everyone else is no, that is not required. What is required is a high level of expectations for the learning for all students.

> Research on scripted or programmed instruction indicates that the rate of learning is far less than average, with an effect size of 0.23.

At the conclusion of this meeting, Ms. Garber and her colleagues agree on the expectations they have of their learners. It should not matter which English teacher you have; all of them should provide experiences designed to allow students to master the content. This is equity in action. However, as you will soon see, the second and third questions in the PLC+ framework not only allow for but demand that teachers adjust their approach to teaching based on where their students are and what is needed to move the learning forward. The destination is the same; the paths toward that destination may differ.

Ms. Garber's response to her early-career colleague is both direct and representative of the vision, mission, and goals of a PLC+. She responds, "No. Our job is to agree on what students need to learn. How they learn it will depend on where your learners are when they walk through that door." Just because you have the same analysis, learning intentions, and success criteria does not mean the classrooms have to look the same each and every day. After all, our learners are not the same.

THE PROFESSIONAL LEARNING OF A PLC+

Before we move forward in the conversation, we want to take a moment to look at the *professional learning* component of the successful PLC+. Where does professional learning come into play during this part of the framework? As we engage in answering the question "Where are we going?" there is a high likelihood that this deliberate, intentional, and purposeful look at the standards/curriculum expectations, and then the development of learning intentions and success criteria, causes discomfort. Individual teachers' comfort level or ability to truly know where we are going might be inhibited by their content knowledge. Say, for example, one of the second-grade teachers has had a change in grade-level assignment, and is not familiar with how to support younger students in developing their algebraic thinking. This teacher can then engage in professional learning to close his or her own content knowledge gap. However, the teacher's learning can be accelerated in the company of a PLC+ team that is committed to examining grade-specific standards/curriculum expectations. PLC+ teams that embrace collective efficacy will naturally offer new members of their learning community support in ways such as explaining concepts or showing how the content is organized, as well as demonstrating how to scaffold thinking so that they all have a good sense of what needs to be taught.

> It should not matter which English teacher you have; all of them should provide experiences designed to allow students to master the content. This is equity in action.

As we will see in subsequent examinations of other components of the PLC+ framework, professional learning needs may extend beyond content knowledge and into pedagogical content knowledge, equity, and facilitation. These areas will be addressed in upcoming chapters. For now, PLC+ teams should use this component of the framework to ensure each member of the team has the necessary content knowledge to truly know where learners are going and the content needed to get them there. The activator, and the entire PLC+ team as a whole, should be on the lookout for signs of confusion or lack of content knowledge. Some teachers may not feel comfortable sharing what they don't understand, because doing so takes quite a bit of trust. Over time, this dissipates, as team members come to understand that we all have gaps in our knowledge and that it is in our collective best interest to help each other develop a deep understanding of the learning students need to do.

CONCLUSION

When considering the reply to the question "Where are we going?" PLC+ teams must ground themselves in a collective process of developing a clear understanding of what their students are expected to know, understand, and be able to do as articulated by their national or state/provincial standards or curriculum expectations. This requires analysis of the standards/expectations to develop clear learning intentions and success criteria. Teachers will utilize their analysis of the standards to develop learning progressions, which lead to learning intentions and success criteria that communicate to students what they are expected to know, understand, and be able to do.

To ensure that we are creating an inclusive learning environment that provides equity of access to all learners, we must also establish consistent expectations for each student. In this chapter, we identified how teams can engage in this continual process of knowing "Where are we going" by intimately knowing the standards/curriculum expectations of the grade and subjects they teach. We believe, in order to provide equity and high expectations for all students, PLC+ teams should use this component of the framework through a facilitated approach to ensure each member of the team has the necessary content knowledge to truly know where learners are going and the content needed to get them there. Listed below are critical areas to this component of the framework that have been highlighted in this chapter:

> Professional learning needs may extend beyond content knowledge and into pedagogical content knowledge, equity, and facilitation.

- Analyzing the standards/curriculum expectations

- Providing equity in access and opportunity for learning

- Outlining learning progressions

- Developing learning intentions and success criteria

- Moving beyond a single instructional day

In addition, answering this question builds on the four crosscutting values that are included in the PLC+ framework. The following table provides summary information for each as well as reflective questions teams can discuss.

EQUITY	Establishing a clear understanding of what students need to learn helps prevent teachers from being inequitable and partial. The rigor level and expectations of the standard remain the constant, yet the pathway for how students arrive at mastery of the standard/curriculum expectation can look different. <ul><li>How does your PLC+ currently determine the level of rigor for differentiated learning opportunities for all students against the established learning intentions and success criteria?</li><li>Does your PLC+ team engage in culturally responsive teaching? What is the evidence that you have done so?</li><li>What strategies does your PLC+ use to support students at different readiness levels in attaining mastery of the learning intention?</li><li>How can analyzing the standard or curriculum expectation to understand the expectations contained therein help ensure equitable outcomes for all students?</li><li>In what ways do content, language, and social learning intentions support equity?</li></ul>
HIGH EXPECTATIONS	Analyzing standards/curriculum expectations and looking at the skills and concepts within them drive design of learning intentions and success criteria for students. These represent nonnegotiable components of learning for all students and ensure appropriate expectations are set for every learner. <ul><li>How do you currently use learning intentions and success criteria to ensure design of rigorous learning tasks?</li><li>In what ways can clear learning intentions and measurable success criteria help close learning opportunity gaps?</li></ul>

INDIVIDUAL AND COLLECTIVE EFFICACY	Working together within your PLC+ to review standards/expectations, pacing guides, and resources—as well as to analyze standards and develop learning intentions, success criteria, and learning progressions—allows for strong collaboration to learn and grow from each other. Working collaboratively provides opportunities for PLC+ members to tap into the collective expertise of the team as a whole and determine ways in which all students will achieve the targeted objectives. • In what ways does analyzing the standards build collective efficacy in your PLC+? • How does your PLC+ currently determine "where they are going"? • What strategies does your PLC+ currently use to involve students in the process of understanding the established learning intentions and success criteria? • In what ways do learning intentions and success criteria link to the other components involved in teaching and learning?
ACTIVATION	Keeping a PLC+ focused on what students need to know rather than what is neat to know requires an activator to keep the team focused. Teams can digress very easily when determining what all students must be expected to learn. Getting off topic and digressing stifles the efficiency of the PLC+ and takes away their ability to keenly focus on what students need to learn, as well as on the evidence that will demonstrate they have done so. • How do you currently employ facilitation strategies in your PLC+ structure? • What strengths does your PLC+ have around facilitation? • What opportunities does your PLC+ have around facilitation? • What facilitation strategies does your PLC+ use to determine whether all members understand "Where are we going?" • What opportunities does your PLC+ provide to build content knowledge?

QUESTION	MY THOUGHTS	OUR COLLECTIVE THOUGHTS
Did we plan from grade-level-appropriate standards?		
How did we address all parts of the standard(s) in our learning progression?		
In what ways will the learning progression apply to all students?		
How have we considered accommodations and modifications for students who need them?		
Do we expect all students to reach mastery of the standards?		
In what ways are the tasks we use appropriately rigorous to ensure students have the experiences necessary to master the standards?		
What is our plan to address learning gaps that we identify?		
What is our plan to accelerate student learning as appropriate?		

COLLABORATIVE WORK WITH YOUR TEAM

Module 6:
Equity and Expectations Values Checklist
page 52 in
The PLC+ Playbook

Module 6:
Activate Learning for Myself and Others Checklist
page 53 in
The PLC+ Playbook

Module 6:
Collective Efficacy Checklist
page 54 in
The PLC+ Playbook

ACTIVATE LEARNING FOR MYSELF AND OTHERS CHECKLIST

Student learning needs drive adult learning needs. Once we've established teacher clarity through analysis of standards and through design of learning progressions, learning intentions, and success criteria, teams need to take a step back to reflect on their personal learning. Are there any adult learning needs that must be met to best be able to support student learning? As already discussed, the + in the PLC+ is you, and so it is important to recognize learning for teachers is a constant. Doctors *practice* medicine, lawyers *practice* law. Why should it be any different for teachers? Teaching is a complex profession with many moving parts. Just as you wouldn't want your doctor ignoring advances in medicine and new ways to support health, the same holds true for teachers. We know more today than we did 30 years ago, and we will continue to know more as we move into the future. Absorbing that requires learning.

WHAT ARE THE LEARNING NEEDS OF MY STUDENTS? What do students need to learn?	WHAT ARE MY LEARNING NEEDS SO I CAN MEET MY STUDENTS' LEARNING NEEDS? What strategies might I need to learn more about?	WHAT LEARNING WILL I ENGAGE IN TO MEET MY LEARNING NEEDS? What will I do on my own? What can I do with colleagues?

COLLECTIVE EFFICACY CHECKLIST

Teams that are empowered to make decisions, act, communicate clearly, and hold themselves accountable for their efforts manifest high degrees of collective teacher efficacy (CTE). Use the checklist below to gauge and monitor the actions that will follow your work about the first guiding question, "Where are we going?"

QUESTION	MY THOUGHTS	OUR COLLECTIVE THOUGHTS
Have we made plans to visit each other's classrooms to focus on teaching *and* learning? Are we willing to challenge each other to become stronger in our craft?		
How will we share the work we have done with others in the school?		
Do we have confidence in our ability to guide all students to meet standards?		
Are we prepared and committed to take action to move student learning forward? How will we accomplish this?		

PLC+ Framework Guiding Questions

1. **Where are we going?**
2. **Where are we now?**
3. **How do we move learning forward?**
4. **What did we learn today?**
5. **Who benefited and who did not benefit?**

THE STORY BEHIND THE QUESTION

Having established learning intentions, success criteria, and learning progressions, PLC+ teams can begin to engage in initial assessment of student learning through work samples, student interviews, and initial assessments. After all, there is no point in teaching something that students already know. There is considerable evidence that valuable classroom time is spent on content that students have already mastered (e.g., Engel, Claessens, & Finch, 2013). However, this particular question is prone to biases about student learning and particular groups of students. Thus, the effective navigation of this question requires us to be aware of those biases and recognize them when they infiltrate the PLC+ collaborative team meeting.

Effective activation and facilitation of this particular question focuses on eliminating "noise" in the world of teachers. Activators help keep the PLC+ conversations focused, productive, and objective. Teachers don't ever talk about having too much time on their

Video 4
Introduction to Chapter 3

resources.corwin.com/
plcplus

hands, and effective facilitation supports efficiency within the PLC+ so that there is time for reflection and continuous improvement as well as time to be action oriented in response to the data.

Equity applies to teaching and learning such that it allows a PLC+ to address a number of biases, whether they are conscious or unconscious. Unaddressed biases and assumptions leave professional learning communities at risk of missing certain students' learning gaps while wasting the time of others by limiting their ability to grow and develop. While these conversations may initially feel uncomfortable, they are a necessary component of an effective PLC+.

> Equity allows a PLC+ to address a number of biases, whether they are conscious or unconscious. Unaddressed biases and assumptions leave professional learning communities at risk of missing certain students while wasting the time of others.

Ensuring a constant focus on high **expectations** for all students not only requires knowledge about the skills and concepts students to need to master, it also calls for teachers to determine the knowledge students already bring to the learning experience, as well as to identify any current specific learning gaps that are present. A PLC+ team's ability to do this recaptures instructional time lost to teaching concepts students already know, and helps the teachers build on students' assets to support a deeper level of learning.

There is an incredible power that can be capitalized when a PLC+ not only is individually efficacious, but seeks ways to build positive interdependence through **collective efficacy**. While there are certain factors that teachers have no control over, there is much that they do to positively impact student learning.

A PLC+ TEAM IN ACTION

Gina Johnston is facilitating her team's conversation on teaching their fourth-grade students how to identify themes in literature. This is their second collaborative team meeting this week, as they are deep into planning learning experiences for their students. They have identified where they need to go with students' learning and have collected data about their students' current understanding of the standards. They have analyzed and organized their data and are spending this time talking about students' needs. The standard requires that students both determine the theme and summarize the text. This learning is new to their students, and so the teachers administered a brief initial assessment to determine students' strengths and needs around this learning.

The fourth graders were given two passages to read and were asked to identify the major themes from the text as well as to write summaries of the text. One text's theme was more obvious than the other. Before asking the students to do this, the teachers briefly defined *theme* for their students so that the assessment would not be influenced by lack of definitional knowledge. For example, Marco Espinosa said to his students, "Today, we're going to read two passages, and then you'll have a chance to answer some questions, including a couple of questions about theme. The theme is the life lesson of a story or the author's main message to the reader. When I think about this, I think it's the message I remember a few hours after reading. So, if my friend said to me, 'What did the author want you to know?' my answer would not be all of the details, but really would be the major message. The other thing you'll notice on this assessment is that you're asked to summarize. That is not new, and I know that you all know how to write really strong summaries. Remember, this is for me to figure out what to teach, so try your best but don't stress over it."

In analyzing the results of the initial assessment, another teacher on the team, Kristen Cavanaugh, shared with the group, "All of my students demonstrated mastery of the part of the standard that required a summary. I think that unit we taught on explanatory writing a few months ago was really powerful because they still get it. I have four students who were really strong on theme, but the rest were not. How about all of you?"

When teachers experience success with their peers, teacher collective efficacy is built and reinforced. Their conversation continued as they shared students' current performance levels. It turns out that across the grade level, there were only four students who really did not

COLLABORATIVE WORK WITH YOUR TEAM

Module 7:
Sample Student Feedback Survey
page 57 in
The PLC+ Playbook

produce an acceptable summary. And there were very few students who demonstrated mastery of theme. In other words, the vast majority of students did not need additional instruction on summarizing, while almost all of them needed instruction on theme.

Ms. Johnston's team knows that they need to fully analyze their data and determine quality inferences into student learning before they jump into solving the problems presented by the initial assessment. They decide to create a grid of student performance across the grade level so that they can develop plans to ensure that all students' learning needs are met. As Ms. Johnston says, "We used to skip this step, but now we realize how critical it is to spend time talking about our students' current level of performance as well as the factors that may have contributed to their success and needs. When we didn't do that, we missed some students and wasted time for others. We're much more precise now, and it really doesn't take that long to get this right."

DEFICIT THINKING

When we explore where kids are now there is a potential risk of engaging in deficit thinking.

Before we dive too much deeper into the process of data mining, we would like to acknowledge the potential risk in exploring where students are now in their learning journey. That risk is in engaging in deficit thinking. When teachers examine data about what students cannot currently do, they run the risk of thinking that those students will never be able to do it. Or they end up with low expectations for students in the belief that a little growth is good enough. As Valencia (2012) noted, "Deficit thinking blames the victim for school failure, instead of examining structural factors, such as segregation and inequities in school financing, that prevent low-SES [socio-economic status] students of color from achieving." Importantly, it's not just students who live in poverty or those who are from traditionally underrepresented groups that can be victims of deficit thinking. Here is where deficit thinking can literally paralyze a team and keep them from moving forward. Horn and Little (2010) noted that when teachers positioned themselves based on a challenge they were facing as helpless based on circumstances beyond their control, teams most often did not look to any solutions. In part, that is why we believe that teams need skilled facilitators, or as we call them *activators*. One of the roles of the activator is to be aware of the potential for deficit thinking and to address it when it arises. Lindsey, Jungwirth, Pahl, and Lindsay (2009) describe a technique whereby facilitators use breakthrough questions to help a team shift their thinking to an inquiry approach, changing the dynamic and causing the team to consider possibilities, rather than assigning blame.

Coming up with useful questions often involves noting the difference between the sphere of influence and the sphere of concern. For example, another team at a school in the same district as Ms. Johnston was stuck on teaching place value in mathematics to its second graders. The data were not good, and the vast majority of students did not reach proficiency in this unit. In the course of their discussion, the talk turned to parents. One of the teachers said, "If we had more parent help at home, I think that they would have done better.

> Coming up with useful questions often involves noting the difference between the sphere of influence and the sphere of concern.

"I agree," another said. "And the fact is that most are still learning English. It's hard to learn mathematics in another language."

At that point, the activator interjected, "Let's take a closer look at what we think might have caused this. It seems that there are some things that we can control and other things that we can't control." She then asked a breakthrough question. "Based on our current results, if we were teaching this unit again, what might we do differently?"

This question gave the team pause. After a few moments of silence, one teacher ventured, "The vocabulary was challenging. I'd put a greater emphasis on teaching the math vocabulary more explicitly to those who need it." Her colleague responded, "That's a good point. We have their language proficiency data. We already know who needs more vocab support."

As the team continued their work, they realized that there were many things that were within their control. This process, and the strong facilitation skills, moved them out of deficit thinking into a deeper understanding of the students' current needs.

INITIAL ASSESSMENTS

Assessment drives instruction, and it begins with the initial assessment at the beginning of the year, which helps us identify where students are in their learning and where we need to begin. But the start of the year is not the only time that initial assessments are useful. For each unit of study, teams review students' current level of understanding and skill and may administer additional initial assessments. For example, when moving from a unit of study on cells to ecology in biology, the teachers administered an initial assessment, because they had no other information about students' level of understanding. But rather than administer a new assessment, a group of English teachers reviewed students' writing progress from the previous unit to identify strengths and needs that they would continue to address in the upcoming unit.

Every year there are there are variables in play that cannot be fully known, especially background knowledge and prior experience. Knowledge is power. When PLC+ teams move forward instructionally without this knowledge about their students' current state of learning, valuable instructional time is wasted. There are two inherent dangers. The first is teaching students concepts and skills they already know. The second error is overlooking knowledge gaps, and therefore failing to address potential stumbling blocks. The first error is more common; the second perpetuates an inequitable educational system.

It has been estimated that somewhere between 30 and 40 percent of instructional minutes are wasted teaching students things they already know. Without initial assessments, it is nearly impossible to streamline instruction and repurpose time to close knowledge and skills gaps.

Initial assessments, which are part of a formative assessment system, don't need to be particularly long and elaborate, as Gail Johnston's team illustrated with their assessment on students' knowledge of theme and summary. But it isn't always necessary for teams to create special assessments. For example, the professional learning community composed of the eighth-grade teachers at First Avenue Middle School used the results of the last informational writing task to inform their conversation about where to go next. This PLC+ meets in "houses"—cross-curricular teams that share the same students. Social studies teacher Alexis Bartram noted that the summative data from the social studies reports the students wrote on the abolitionist movement in the United States showed that a significant percentage of them struggled with elaboration of evidence.

> It has been estimated that somewhere between 30 and 40 percent of instructional minutes are wasted teaching students things they already know.

Science teacher Mike Leonard responded, "That's really interesting. This next unit in my class is on traits and mutations. They'll be writing a report on the mutations of an organism of their choice. Can you share the details with me, so I have a better sense of what I'm going to need to teach them about this writing element? I need to dive deeper into the data and zero in on the instructional need. I wonder what the barriers for their learning have been and how we can help them learn more this time we focus on writing."

At other times, it is the content knowledge students possess that is of primary interest. Teaching a new topic requires students to explore what they know and don't know. Topic-specific initial assessments are often included in the publisher's curriculum materials and can be useful if they are aligned with the learning intentions and success criteria, and provide PLC+ teams the right evidence to make strong inferences they can then act upon.

There are also other easy methods for gathering information about what students already know. The ninth-grade algebra team at Mountain Springs High School administers a short version of their end-of-unit test before the new unit begins. In preparation for an upcoming unit on exponential growth, students worked in teams to attempt to solve a problem about the growth of bacteria in the mouth when a person forgets to brush his or her teeth. (A similar problem will appear on the summative assessment a few weeks from now.) The math teachers listen in on the mathematical reasoning as students wrestle with how they might figure out how many bacteria have replicated in two minutes, four minutes, and eight minutes. The teachers use the same chart to capture key mathematical practices, tallying the number of times they witness students using models, making sense of problems, and using abstract and quantitative reasoning. As Ernesto Flores, one of the algebra teachers, explained, "It's less about whether they come up with the correct answer, and more about to what extent they are applying what they already know about functions, as well as mathematical thinking, to figure out how to tackle the problem." The team met to compare and discuss results and then formulated a plan to address anticipated needs for the upcoming unit (which requires moving to the next question, addressed in Chapter 4).

To our thinking, an effective professional learning community uses such initial assessments of students' current learning before moving

> To our thinking, an effective professional learning community uses such initial **assessments** of students' current learning before moving their discussion to actions that they can take to increase learning.

their discussion to actions that they can take to increase learning. When we skip the initial assessment and rely on post-assessment data only, we have evidence that students learned but not that they learned from us. And, importantly, the whole point of engaging in the PLC+ process is to impact students' learning through our collective process of learning how to teach to meet their needs.

Let's now turn our attention to data collection and data review, as these protocols can help teams focus their conversations on students' current levels of mastery.

ANALYZING FOR EQUITY GAPS

Before we explore data protocols, it's important to recognize that the information we gather from assessments and other sources will likely reveal equity gaps. Specifically engaging in discourse to root out equity gaps for language learners, socioeconomic status, disability status, and learners of different races and ethnicities is the foundation for engaging in productive dialogue during PLC+ meetings. If only aggregate, whole-grade-level, or content-area data are discussed, then gaps in learning might be masked, leaving teams ill equipped to address institutional barriers and inequitable instructional practices.

Having said that, the data need to be disaggregated in multiple ways to ensure that patterns can be identified. Some argue that we should focus on individual students and not the categories that define one of their characteristics (such as gender, race and ethnicity, socioeconomic status, disability and linguistic status, or cultural background). However, the problem is that doing so may prevent teams from talking about structural and institutional barriers to learning that may require administrative interventions. Some of the barriers will likely be instructional and curricular in nature. Examples of structural and institutional barriers include tracking, access to college preparatory (AP/IB) coursework, disproportionalities in suspension rates, disciplinary referrals, and referrals to special education, to name a few. Formal descriptive categories make it possible for teams to disaggregate data and respond to inequitable results. But consider the problems that can arise when no one bothers, or the team simply does not take the time, to examine disaggregated data, such as the portion of the student body who attend the magnet program at the school and travel longer distances to attend. Now imagine talking about individual students and developing a tutoring program for them, only to find out that the group has a different transportation schedule and can't attend the new program. Situations like this, and worse, occur all of the time when teams fail to analyze data for patterns. The antidote is ensuring your PLC+ team starts with collecting initial assessments of students' learning.

DATA COLLECTION

The PLC+ thrives on the data it gathers. It can also perish if the data aren't used to take action, or if it obscures needs that are hiding in plain sight. The first problem is one that too many schools find themselves mired in. The uptick in data-gathering sources using a variety of digital analysis tools has resulted in what one administrator aptly described as "a tsunami of data." Results of state assessments, measures of school climate, and parent and community engagement surveys can mean that teachers and leaders can become quickly overwhelmed. In the face of data overload, is it any wonder that the results—coded in too many multicolored tables and passed out at a planning week meeting in August—are then relegated to a binder that sits unused behind a teacher's desk?

So what kinds of data are useful for a PLC+? Broad-scan assessments do have some value. They can provide useful information about past progress of students (state assessments), serve as a snapshot of the emotional tone of the school (climate data), and highlight underutilized resources (parent and community engagement surveys). In professional learning communities, these data sources can further illuminate trends that are occurring at the classroom level. But we would like to highlight several general types of data that are especially useful for a PLC+ for uncovering academic and nonacademic information about students:

- Analysis of student work samples

- Short interviews with a representative sample of students

> The PLC+ thrives on the data it gathers. It can also perish if the data aren't used to take action, or if it obscures needs that are hiding in plain sight.

- Initial and end-of-unit assessment results
- Student climate surveys
- Student feedback about a completed unit of study

Developing a Data Collection Plan

These data collection efforts can become overwhelming if there isn't a plan for gathering and analyzing it. Teachers at Loma Portia Elementary School create a data collection checklist whenever they make a decision to gather information.

"The first question we ask ourselves is about our purpose," said teacher Kiley Desmond. "If we're not clear ourselves, we can end up wasting a lot of time." As a team, they identify the types of data that they will collect. Importantly, the data are not just collected for team meetings. Teachers also collect data that they can use formatively to move learning forward. Some of the data are used during team meetings. For example, they decided to collect writing samples and running records. The running records were used formatively to track students' progress, and teachers discussed the progress during their meetings, but adjusted instruction almost daily based on the data. The writing samples were also used to gauge impact, but, as Ms. Desmond said, "Writing doesn't change each day like we see with reading development, so let's collect writing less often and then meet together to analyze the writing."

Literacy coach Sarita Rosales added, "We learned the hard way that it was too easy to walk away from a collaborative team meeting thinking we had a plan, only to realize a week later that we really weren't sure what our agreements were."

Watching for Inequities

The second potential problem with data collection is that a PLC+ team can have a narrow definition of its charge and therefore

COLLABORATIVE WORK
WITH YOUR TEAM

Module 7:
Making Decisions
About Data

page 60 in
The PLC+ Playbook

overlook inequities that have become the fabric of the school. This can be particularly true when it comes to interrogating systems that perpetuate inequitable educational opportunities. A professional learning community at Westside Union High School was formed to take a detailed look at procedures that reinforced tracking. The team was composed of administrators, counselors, and teachers. Their common challenge was, "How are opportunities to learn rigorous academic content promoted and denied at Westside?"

In order to ensure they weren't missing possible sources of inequities, the team collected data from a wide range of sources. For example, two members of the team interviewed a sample of students about how they made decisions about their course schedules. The two counselors on the team took on the task of surveying parents about their aspirations for their children. The principal pulled the master schedule data, including course offerings and enrollments, reporting them according to a variety of demographic descriptors. The four teachers on the team polled teachers in their respective departments about their observations about the academic demands of the courses they taught.

While the complexities of addressing institutional barriers at the high school would take months of work, the team's initial data collection served as a catalyst to enact change. The data help inform the team members where to look and what options should be considered to provoke the desired change. In time, the master schedule was changed to enhance opportunities to learn, compensatory tutoring programs were established to prepare students for more rigorous course work, and "college knowledge" nights were scheduled to help parents complete paperwork so their children could apply for scholarships, grants, and financial aid.

DATA GATHERING

Depending on the results of your team time discussions, you are likely to need additional time for gathering the data. If the data needed are not immediately available, develop a list of tasks so that the data will be made available for the next meeting. Be sure to charge specific team members with gathering the data the team members agreed they needed.

DATA NEEDED	WHO WILL GATHER IT	DATE NEEDED

COLLABORATIVE WORK WITH YOUR TEAM

Module 7:
Data Gathering
page 61 in
The PLC+ Playbook

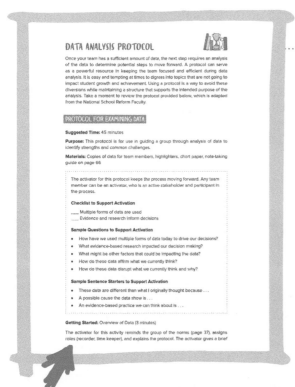

COLLABORATIVE WORK WITH YOUR TEAM

Module 8:
Data Analysis Protocol
page 64 in
The PLC+ Playbook

DATA ANALYSIS PROTOCOLS

Once useful data have been collected, teams need a process to discuss that data. Before we move into data analysis protocols, let's first recognize that teams can get bogged down in this process. If we spend all of our time analyzing data, we don't move to action and thus impact learning. Teams need to strive to focus just enough time to identify trends and patterns that they can use to make learning better. There are several protocols for analyzing and discussing data, but we commonly use one that was adapted from the National School Reform Faculty.

Here's how the third-grade team at Desert View Elementary School drew on this protocol to identify students' levels of understanding about the idea that plants and animals have structures that serve different functions in growth, survival, and reproduction. The initial assessment information, collected using an Internet-based quiz tool, indicated that students had minimal understandings about this concept. Shanice Harris facilitated the group's thinking about their data. She asked Vishnu Agarwa to serve as the recorder and Mindy Schwartz to serve as timekeeper. Ms. Harris then turned the group's attention to the topic, namely students' understanding of the science standard that would guide their unit development. Ms. Harris asked, "What parts of the data caught your attention? Remember, focus on the facts that we see in the data."

Initial Observations on Data

The team then got to work, writing comments on the data. They worked individually, processing their ideas and looking for patterns. After two minutes, Ms. Schwartz announced that time was up, and the group started sharing their thinking. They noted that students did the best on questions related to survival but not so well on growth or reproduction. They also noted that there were no differences between boys and girls, and that the average performance of students who lived in poverty was one point below the average of those who did not. Ms. Schwartz noted, "There isn't a gap based on poverty, because one point wouldn't be significant, but I do see a gap with African American students and Latinx students. African Americans did the best on this whole assessment. At some point, I'd like to talk about why that is, but I know that we have to stay focused on the data right now." Notice that Ms. Schwartz is serving as an activator for this PLC+. She notes the gap in learning for their African American students and Latinx students, but does not allow her team to perseverate on this single issue at this time. Instead, she activates the collaborative dialogue to continue focusing on the data and reserving inferences for after they have analyzed all of the data. In this situation, the role of the activator is paramount to avoid consuming an inordinate amount of time commenting on every issue raised by the data, at the time the issue appears, before getting a full picture of the data.

The role of the activator is paramount to avoid consuming an inordinate amount of time commenting on every issue raised by the data.

Inferences From Data

As they ran out of things to say, Ms. Harris moved their discussion to the next phase saying, "What do the data tell us? What do the data *not* tell us? This is where we get to look at the implications of the data."

The team members returned to their individual data pages and started taking notes. When time was up, Ms. Schwartz asked the group if she could share first. They nodded and she commented, "I think that the data tell us we need to slow down this unit a bit. I'm not sure that the students understood the term *structures*. If they missed that, it would be hard to answer these questions." The group processed this comment and added other inferences from the data.

Ms. Harris then moved the conversation from learning gaps to items to celebrate. Mr. Agarwa was the first to share, saying, "My first thought is that we don't have evidence that students held a lot of misconceptions about this information. They just don't have the content knowledge yet. That's actually easier than trying to address misconceptions. But I noticed that they chose the distractors fairly evenly, so that tells me that there isn't a common misunderstanding." Distractors are incorrect responses, typically within multiple-choice questions; these allow us to diagnose student errors and provide guidance about student misunderstandings. In this case, there was no pattern to the students' wrong answers—they just lacked basic content knowledge.

Laura Torres, another member of the team, added, "It's also good news that we have every student answering all of the questions. Look, the number of responses is the same for all of them. A few months ago, the numbers would trail off as the assessment continued. I think we've really increased their stamina."

Implications for Instructional Practice

When they had exhausted this question, Ms. Harris turned the conversation to problems of practice. "I'm interested in our common challenge. What do we think we need to focus on?" The team was quick to discuss the lack of background knowledge about plant and animal adaptation. They agreed that developing and activating background knowledge would be their common challenge. From there, the team focused on the factors that might have contributed to their problem.

Among these factors, the team identified the students' limited experience with science instruction in the primary grades, a lack of instructional materials aligned to the new standards, insufficient levels of rigor, low levels of engagement and thus motivation for students, lack of relevancy of the content, and challenges with academic language. Ms. Harris then turned their attention to actions they could take based on groups of students they had identified.

The first to speak was Ms. Schwartz, who said, "I'm thinking we need to get students reading more. If we could change their independent reading choices to focus more on adaptation across a wide range of plants and animals, then we could talk about trends students see in the texts they are reading. They would also learn a lot of academic language from this as well." The team agreed and Ms. Harris said that she would contact the librarian to create book boxes for each classroom so that students could read independently and build their background knowledge.

Mr. Agarwa added, "I'd like to encourage a stronger focus in the primary grades on science, which will help future students. We could also plan some hands-on experiences for students now to see adaptation firsthand. I'd be happy to plan that for all of us, if you agree." They did. They also noted that they needed to build their science pedagogical knowledge and agreed to discuss this further at a future meeting.

Tracking Results

It is also important for teams to talk about how they will know if their hypotheses were correct. If a hypothesis is correct, the interventions enacted should result in the expected change. That means that teams need to figure out data collection systems that extend beyond the initial assessment and then plan time to talk about the results of those assessments with one another. In other words, the evidence of student learning needs to be examined against the teachers' practice to see if the practice had the intended result.

ADDRESSING BIAS IN DATA COLLECTION AND ANALYSIS

Underlying every decision about what we choose to gather data on is an unspoken decision about what we won't look at. It is impractical to gather data on everything, and we aren't suggesting that the majority of a PLC+ team's time should be consumed with doing so.

> Underlying every decision about what we choose to gather data on is an unspoken decision about what we won't look at.

But it is crucial to keep conversations about bias at the forefront when making choices about what we examine, and why. These serve as barriers to the change we want to create.

- *Confirmation bias* is the tendency we all have to search for evidence that aligns with our current understanding of a situation. Examining the math grades of students who scored 700 or above on the SAT isn't likely to yield much useful information to the math PLC+, although it is likely to perpetuate a perception (which may not be true) that students are doing an amazing job.

- *Semmelweis reflex* is the tendency to reject what doesn't fit into an existing paradigm. For example, the research showing that collective teacher efficacy has the highest influence on student achievement among 250+ influences has prompted a Semmelweis reflex among some educators, who can't believe that the top influence wouldn't be an instructional routine. Showing up with your mind made up about a problem (e.g., "The seventh graders are out of control!"), coupled with a confirmation bias to locate data that support your position while dismissing contrarian data, is a sure combination for failure.

Vividness bias is the tendency to give outsized attention to a phenomenon that may (or may not) be a signal of other problems.

- *Vividness bias* is the tendency to give outsized attention to a phenomenon that may (or may not) be a signal of other problems. A fight on campus between two groups of students may be an indicator of an uptick in gang activity in the area, or it may be an isolated social dispute that got out of hand. But a knee-jerk reaction to shorten the lunch period to prevent future fights may be the result of vividness bias rather than a measured response aligned with the cause.

- *Omission bias* is change for change's sake. In the example above, the principal may have also been motivated by an omission bias to do *something*, as the fight drew the attention of law enforcement and the local media.

- *Academic bias* suggests that certain types of learning are more important than others. For example, excluding social and emotional learning as factors of academic learning and only focusing on testable content shows academic bias. Beginning an initiative to teach study skills to middle school students without considering the developmental, emotional, and affective needs of students is another example, and doing it is likely to be unsuccessful. A PLC+ that narrows its focus exclusively to cognitive aspects of student learning is overlooking vital information about students.

- *Protectionism* is an unwillingness to accept responsibility or ask for help due to a misguided belief that it is a sign of weakness. In our attempts to protect ourselves or others, we close off opportunities to grow and learn.

- *The echo chamber* is the phenomenon that can occur when a PLC+ relies exclusively on the voices of its members, never consulting with students and community members about important issues.

Implicit Bias

The most challenging bias we all face is implicit bias, defined as sub-conscious and unconscious stereotype-confirming thoughts based on factors of race, gender, sexual orientation, age, ability, cultural background, and socioeconomic status. Implicit bias lies below the surface of conscious thought and influences our worldview and the decisions we make. They are based on the patterns and generalizations our brain makes in observing the world, which is what your brain is supposed to do. But as Payne, Niemi, and Doris (2018) note, implicit biases "set people up to overgeneralize, sometimes leading to discrimination even when people feel they are being fair" (p. 1).

Implicit bias lies below the surface of conscious thought and influences our worldview and the decisions we make.

The Yale University Center for Teaching and Learning suggests that educators take steps to mitigate implicit bias in their own work. The first is to engage in reflective teaching practices that promote critical self-analysis. Reflective teaching practices include journaling and teaching inventories. The second is cultivating inclusivity through professional development about cultural proficiency. A third strategy is soliciting feedback from others, especially peers and students. In addition, members of a PLC+ can build the habit of interrogating the team's implicit bias by using questions about decisions.

Mashaun Sutton, the activator for the mathematics PLC+ at Walt Whitman Middle School, had worked in concert with other members, who were interested in strengthening feedback mechanisms in their classes. As part of this effort, all of the teachers had surveyed their students to ask them about how they got help in class. The team's analysis of the data found that their female students were less likely to seek help than male classmates. In an effort to change this dynamic, the PLC+ team discussed possible actions they could take, including having students complete entrance slips at the beginning of the lesson to note what help might be needed.

Mr. Sutton said, "So let's dig down about this proposed action. We know there's always the possibility of some unintended consequences, so let's check ourselves." Mr. Sutton looked at the protocol the PLC+ used to check for bias, and posed questions to the team. He asked them whether the entrance slip system might:

- Exclude any students?

- Make assumptions about any students that may be unwarranted?

- Assume greater (or lesser) competence than was evidenced?

- Apply equitable solutions for all students?

The third question sparked discussion among the team about a few of their students who had more difficulty with writing on demand. "I'm thinking about Letrice [a student with a learning disability]," offered math teacher Dell Whitlock. "She's quiet, she's not confident in her abilities, but she's one of those students who would benefit from more peer feedback. But if she had to write an entrance slip every morning, I think it might shut her down." Several other teachers nodded in agreement, thinking of students on their own roster with learning and disposition profiles similar to that of Letrice. The team agreed that while the idea was a good one, they needed to consider alternative ways to elicit this kind of information from specific students. At Mr. Sutton's encouragement, the PLC+ team agreed that they would try the entrance slips for one week, and augment them by checking in directly with two students who might find the written form daunting. "Let's check in with each other this week to see what we're finding out," said Mr. Sutton.

> While bias can never be totally eliminated, the conscious application of questions to interrogate bias improves the team's ability to gain an accurate reply to the question, "Where are we now?"

As a quick note, this particular team decided to rotate through one-on-one student conferences in place of written entrance slips. This allowed learners to engage in more direct feedback with the teachers at some times, and complete the written entrance ticket at other times.

Teams who collect, analyze, and act upon data always risk that any one of a number of biases might occur. But wise PLC+ members are conscious of their biases, or at least have an awareness of the potential for bias, and check themselves to see whether their decisions might be influenced by a bias. While bias can never be totally eliminated, the conscious application of questions to interrogate bias improves the team's ability to gain an accurate reply to the question "Where are we now?" In addition, active examination of a variety of biases increases the likelihood that the PLC+ team's actions will be equitable ones that uphold high expectations.

IDENTIFYING THE COMMON CHALLENGE

Teams seem to work better when they have a common goal (e.g., Cockerell, 2008). Shared goals allow members of the team to allocate their resources, including time, to achieving the goal. Goals are important, as they serve as a public acknowledgment of the direction a team is taking. However, goals cannot simply be imposed on teams. Doing so compromises the commitment that some members will have to achieving the goal. When team members develop and agree on a shared goal, there is an increased likelihood that everyone will work toward achieving that goal.

In the PLC+ framework, we focus on a common challenge that serves as the goal that the team wants to accomplish. We use the term *common challenge*, as we have found it to be more inviting than *problem of practice* or *SMART goal*. In this chapter, two different teams shared their common challenge. They were not told what the common challenge was, but rather identified the common challenge after answering the first two guiding questions. When teams understand where they are going and where they are now, they identify gaps. Often, there are many gaps, and any one of them could serve as the common challenge. In other words, there is no one right common challenge that a team can choose, but there are probably incorrect or time-wasting common challenges that a team could select. When practitioners shared and collectively identified common concerns, or sets of problems, it ignited both their efforts and their passions to deepen their knowledge and expertise by ongoing interaction toward a common goal (Wenger, McDermott, & Snyder, 2002).

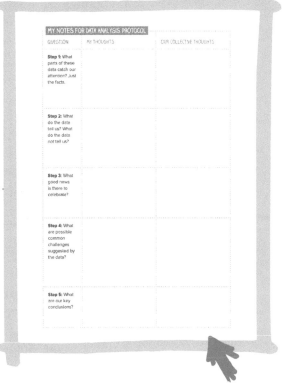

COLLABORATIVE WORK WITH YOUR TEAM

Module 8:
My Notes for Data Analysis Protocol
page 66 in
The PLC+ Playbook

For example, a team of kindergarten teachers identified a gap between what their students needed to learn and what they already knew, and noted that letter formation while writing was very poor. They also noted that most students had a hard time rereading what they had written and seemed to tell listeners about their writing from memory and not from looking at the page. In addition, they noted that students did not have good control of spaces between words. There are any number of common challenges that could have been developed from these data points. What's important is that this group of teachers agreed on a common challenge and then set forth to address that challenge. In this case, they decided that their challenge was "if we improve students' mastery of print conventions, they will be able to reread what they have written."

When attempting to identify a common challenge, we use the following as a guide:

1. **The common challenge is grounded in the evidence we gather during the "Where are we now?" phase.** Far too often, teams have a solution or target and look for confirming evidence. For example, the fifth-grade team at Kennedy Elementary believed that they needed to work on targeting assistance to their intermediate long-term English learners. They came to the collaborative team meeting looking for confirming evidence that it was the case. This is an example of confirmation bias. Luckily, they had an amazing activator who guided them through the process, and they were able to see that there were very few intermediate long-term English learners, and their students who made the least progress were actually those at the highest level of proficiency but who had not yet met the basic skills reclassification criteria. Effective PLC+ teams do not operate with a solution-looking-for-a-problem mindset.

2. **The common challenge is observable and actionable.** This means that data can drive action and be collected to determine whether the challenge has been met and directs the actions of team members.

3. **If acted upon, the common challenge should make a significant difference in students' learning.** After all, our teaching should focus on helping them learn

what they do not already know. This is often referred to as *teaching in the gap:* the gap between what students already know and what they need to know in order to work toward closing the target learning area gap identified previously.

4. **The common challenge should mobilize and motivate teachers to engage in the work required to meet the goals that they have for themselves and their students**. Timperley, Kaser, and Halbert (2014) found that what teachers are professionally curious about increases their motivation, which leads to student achievement. A high-functioning PLC+ team capitalizes on the collective curiosity of its members to focus their inquiry.

Some common challenges include these:

- *Our students generally cannot describe what they are learning or how they will know whether they are successful.*

- *Some students aren't able to identify functions in word problems in math so they can write an equation to solve the problem.*

- *Students are struggling with providing evidence in their writing and not using the claim-evidence-reasons framework.*

- *Ninth-grade students have been identified as being in danger of failing courses their first semester. This is a critical point to intervene and prevent students from losing motivation, failing, and dropping out of school.*

Once the team has a common challenge, they turn their attention to ways to meet that challenge. The obvious place to start is instruction. In some PLC models, teams are discouraged from discussing instruction, because there is a fear that teachers may be told how to teach or because the focus might shift from learning to teaching. The PLC+ model encourages conversations about instructional innovation because teachers need time to share their practices with one another (Timperley, 2011). Teachers also need time to consider what barriers might be hindering learning and to come to know their students as learners and people. Understanding students' cultural backgrounds allows teachers to design instruction that builds on assets and allows students to make personal connections, while keeping the learning at the appropriate level of rigor. Having said

> Once the team has a common challenge, they turn their attention to ways to meet that challenge. The obvious place to start is instruction.

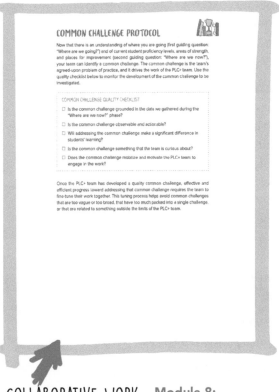

COLLABORATIVE WORK WITH YOUR TEAM

Module 8:
Common
Challenge Protocol
page 67 in
The PLC+ Playbook

COLLABORATIVE WORK WITH YOUR TEAM

Module 8:
Reaching Consensus
on the Common
Challenge
page 69 in
The PLC+ Playbook

that, it's important to note that the practices should have some evidence of impact. and the team should collect evidence to determine whether or not the practice worked for their students.

CONCLUSION

The question "Where are we now?" is the start of a collective process for teams as they take inventory of student strengths and needs, analyze the data, and eventually determine solutions that will address the needs of students. PLC+ teams ground themselves in a collective process of determining a common challenge that is based on student needs evidenced by data. The common challenge should be observable, actionable, and grounded in evidence. The common challenge is best addressed when teams have conversations about the evidence in determining the use of specific approaches or strategies. In the age of accountability, teachers often feel the need to have a quick response to common challenges because of the urgency of improving performance scores. Unfortunately, under such pressure, we may jump to solutions without careful consideration; a lack of consideration occurs when we do not take time to collect and analyze the data, respond to the needs of all learners, and attend to the process of learning itself.

When we jump, we do not increase student performance. We may attempt to meet school improvement goals, and we spend time in teams without a process or space for the collection and analysis of a variety of data that would bring awareness to instructional strategies that address real-time needs for all students. In this chapter, we proposed that PLC+ teams provide this space, allowing teams to carefully consider real-time information about students, teaching, and the learning environment to answer the question "Where are we now?" As a recap, the structural processes your PLC+ team will take to answer this question are as follows:

COLLABORATIVE WORK WITH YOUR TEAM

Module 8:
Common Challenge Tuning Protocol
page 67 in
The PLC+ Playbook

- Collecting initial assessments to guide instructional decisions

- Determining equity gaps from data collection and analysis

- Addressing biases in data collection and analysis

- Identifying a common challenge

In answering this question, the four crosscutting values of a PLC+ are addressed. The following table highlights some of the ways each value is addressed and includes reflection questions useful as teams consider their efforts.

EQUITY	An equity lens applied to teaching and learning allows a PLC+ to address a number of biases, whether they are conscious or unconscious. PLC+ teams run the risk of missing certain students while wasting the time of others when biases or assumptions aren't addressed and talked about. While these conversations may initially feel uncomfortable, they are a necessary component of an effective PLC+. • How do biases potentially damage how we look at student learning? • How does your PLC+ currently evaluate biases included in learning experiences for students? • Why is it important to look at data as an aggregate as well as disaggregated? What are the pros and cons of each? • How does the PLC+ team mitigate against deficit thinking?
HIGH EXPECTATIONS	Ensuring a constant focus on high expectations for all students not only requires knowledge about the skills and concepts students need to master, it also calls on a teacher's ability to determine the knowledge students already bring to the learning experience. A teacher's ability to do this saves instructional time and supports a deeper level of learning for students. • In what ways does your PLC+ currently gather evidence to determine the appropriate entry point for instruction? • How does your PLC+ maintain high expectations when students' readiness for learning varies? • How does your PLC+ communicate high expectations for learning to students?
INDIVIDUAL AND COLLECTIVE EFFICACY	There is an incredible power that can be capitalized on when a PLC+ not only is individually efficacious, but seeks ways to build positive interdependence through collective efficacy. While there are certain factors that teachers have no control over, there is much that they do to positively impact student learning. • How can looking at the sphere of concern and the sphere of influence support navigating through external barriers to student learning? • Does the current climate of your PLC+ enable its members to learn and grow from each other? Why is this? • How can collective efficacy support your PLC+ in its ability to impact all learners?

ACTIVATION	There is a lot of "noise" in the world of teachers. Activators help keep the PLC+ conversations focused, productive, and objective. Teachers don't ever talk about having too much time on their hands, and effective activation supports efficiency within the PLC+ so that there is time to be action oriented in response to the challenges the team identifies.
	• Which initial assessments are useful to determine what students already know?
	• How can you activate hard conversations about data?
	• How do you keep the team focused on the data review rather than hypothesizing solutions?

COLLABORATIVE WORK WITH YOUR TEAM

Module 9:
Equity and Expectations Values Checklist

page 74 in
The PLC+ Playbook

ACTIVATE LEARNING FOR MYSELF AND OTHERS CHECKLIST

Student learning needs drive adult learning needs. Once teams understand where students are now in their learning journey, teams need to take a step back to reflect on their personal learning. Are there any adult learning needs that must be met to best be able to support student learning? As already discussed, the + in the PLC+ is you, and so it is important to recognize learning for teachers is a constant. Based on the trend data and the common challenge, what learning do you (or your team) need to accomplish to ensure that all students are successful?

WHAT ARE THE ADULT LEARNING IMPLICATIONS OF THE COMMON CHALLENGE?	WHAT ARE MY LEARNING NEEDS SO I CAN MEET MY STUDENTS' LEARNING NEEDS? What strategies might I need to learn more about?	WHAT LEARNING WILL I ENGAGE IN TO MEET MY LEARNING NEEDS? What will I do on my own? What can I do with colleagues?

COLLECTIVE EFFICACY CHECKLIST

Teams that are empowered to make decisions, act, communicate clearly, and hold themselves accountable for their efforts manifest high degrees of collective teacher efficacy (CTE). Use the table below to gauge and monitor the actions that will follow your work about the second guiding question, "Where are we now?"

QUESTION	MY THOUGHTS	OUR COLLECTIVE THOUGHTS
In what ways has the data collection and analysis process impacted us? Have we been challenged by what we have found?		
Do we feel confident that collectively we can meet the needs of our students?		
How will we support the decisions our team has made?		
How might the common challenge change our collective work?		

COLLABORATIVE WORK WITH YOUR TEAM

Module 9:
Activate Learning for Myself and Others Checklist
page 75 in
The PLC+ Playbook

COLLABORATIVE WORK WITH YOUR TEAM

Module 9:
Collective Efficacy Checklist
page 76 in
The PLC+ Playbook

QUESTION 3:

How Do We

MOVE
LEARNING

↓

FORWARD?

PLC+ Framework Guiding Questions

1. **Where are we going?**
2. **Where are we now?**
3. **How do we move learning forward?**
4. **What did we learn today?**
5. **Who benefited and who did not benefit?**

THE STORY BEHIND THE QUESTION

Now that we know where we are headed, we can tackle the issue of how to get there At this point, it's time to ask, "How do we move learning forward?" This can be a challenge. Teachers are bombarded with tricks, ideas, and strategies from many different sources. At times, decisions about "what to do on Monday" leave teachers either trying anything or relying on their favorite strategy, without evidence of its impact. This question requires PLC+ collaborative teams to assimilate the answers to the first two questions into a purposeful and intentional decision about what works best to move learning forward. This forward movement could require PLC+ team members to engage in furthering their own professional learning or simply changing their approach to teaching this particular skill or content.

Effective facilitation of this particular question ensures that strategies selected are evidence-based and responsive to the learning needs of students. Many teachers have strategies that they use without knowledge of

Video 5
Introduction to Chapter 4

resources.corwin.com/
plcplus

the research behind them or the impact they can potentially have on student learning. In addition, we have a collective responsibility to ensure teachers actually develop a deep understanding of the essential elements of the strategy picked. The facilitated dialogue focuses on the validity of the selection of specific strategies and addresses the question: Is this the right strategy at the right time? Further, teams discuss the barriers to learning that exist and how to reduce the impact of those barriers. And, as we have emphasized, **equity** of access and opportunity to learning should be at the forefront of the strategies or approaches selected to move learning forward.

Forward movement could require PLC+ team members to engage in furthering their own professional learning or simply changing their approach to teaching this particular skill or content.

As we highlighted in the previous chapter, ensuring a constant focus on high **expectations** for all students not only requires knowledge about the skills and concepts students to need to master, it also calls on a teacher's ability to determine the knowledge and assets students already bring to the learning experience. The expectation that the learners can and will make progress in their learning should be reflected in the strategies or approaches implemented each and every day. Do we design learning experiences in our classrooms with the consistent expectation that all of our students will learn grade-level content? When we purposefully and intentionally make decisions about which evidence-based practice to use in moving learning forward, and we are prepared to make different decisions based on the evidence about our learners' progress, we build both **individual and collective teacher efficacy**.

A PLC+ TEAM IN ACTION

Equipped with an understanding of where students need to go and where they are now, the first-grade team at River View Elementary School turned their conversation to a common challenge they had identified: Students were making errors while reading, many of which were not self-corrected. In tackling the problem of how to move student learning forward in this area, they discussed the need to group students more flexibly and helped each other form needs-based groups based on the data. They also discussed the instructional materials that they would use, and how to model their thinking through a think-aloud approach for students during whole class instruction. They believed that modeling self-correction would provide students with examples that they could use on their own while reading.

As one teacher said, "I was at a conference and the speaker presented research about modeling and said that the research suggests that modeling can build students' surface-level strategic knowledge. I think that's part of our problem here. Our students don't have strategic knowledge, so they aren't self-correcting. I think modeling this could really help, and there is evidence that if we do model for students, their use of the strategy will improve."

As Bree Santiago noted, "We never used to talk about teaching during our team meetings. We talked about what students need to learn, but not how they might best learn it. We were all on our own to figure out the best ways that we knew how teach."

Ms. Santiago's colleague, Amy Hutchison, added, "But we still end up talking about learning. We want to know if we implemented what we learned appropriately. Did it have the desired impact on student learning? We care about their learning, and we know that we need to try to implement practices that are very likely to ensure that students do learn."

This first-grade team focused their discussion on grouping, because there is evidence that the ways teachers use groups significantly impacts student learning. For example, ability grouping has a relatively low effect size of 0.12, while small group learning has an effect size of 0.47. The first-grade team's grouping practices were informed by the results of a large-scale mathematics study of nearly 4,000 kindergarteners who were English learners (Garrett & Hong, 2016). The researchers found that flexible grouping practices were associated with higher levels of teacher expectations and higher student achievement.

As part of their conversation, Ms. Santiago said, "Let's look at my class. I have several students who are still using only meaning, and especially picture clues, to figure out what the text is saying. Remember that this class used to mostly use visual cues, and they guessed words based on whether the words looked about right. But I'm not seeing them use a lot of structure. They aren't checking to make sure that a word is appropriate for the text. I'm thinking that I should model this more. Do you agree?" This generated a lot of discussion about the ways in which Ms. Santiago could model using structures,

> Do we design learning experiences in our classrooms with the consistent expectation that all of our students will learn grade-level content?

and several of the other first-grade teachers indicated that this was also a need for their classes.

Ms. Santiago continued, "I think that will really help. I look forward to modeling how to use structure. Now I'm thinking about the small groups. I have three students who regularly omit words, and I think I'll meet with them as a group while the rest of the class works collaboratively. And then, I think that I have a group of students that need to increase their accuracy. They have the highest number of total errors, and the errors are spread out over all of the types, and it's lowering their accuracy scores."

In response, Ms. Hutchison said, "Can we talk more about the accuracy group? I have probably two groups like that, and I was thinking, when you were talking, that I needed to tackle one type of error at a time. Do you agree? Is that what you plan to do?" This generated a great deal of conversation, but no clear answer. The teachers decided to try it two different ways, generically and targeted, and then compare results after the next collection of running records.

Ms. Santiago said, "This is so cool. We never did this before. We would have just left the collaborative team meeting knowing that we had things to teach and ways to assess, but not a plan to talk about comparing methods to see which one seems to have the better impact."

As part of the PLC+ process, teams of teachers engage with their colleagues in learning about teaching and, importantly, its impact on learning. There are hundreds of strategies that teachers can use to build students' confidence and competence. Some of those strategies work better than others, but there is no one right way to teach. It's just that we all tend to go to our old favorites; these conversations can broaden our repertoires and may allow us to reach students that we did not reach before.

EVIDENCE—BASED INSTRUCTIONAL PRACTICES

There is no one right way to teach, but there are wrong ways. We believe that teachers show up to school and do the very best job that they know how to do. We do not think teachers wake up in the morning and say to themselves, "How can I really mess up those fifth graders today?" The problem is that some teachers know more about quality instruction, or have more experience teaching and determining impact, than others. In some systems, teachers do not talk with their peers about effective instruction and its impact on learning. Instead, they only spend time focused on what students need to learn and how they will know whether students have learned it. Those are two important considerations, but opportunities to talk about the most effective ways to get that learning to occur are often missed. We're not suggesting that everyone teach the same way, but in the PLC+ model, we talk about the evidence for use of specific approaches. This is one of the characteristics of our model that separates it from others; PLC+ teachers collectively learn about teaching to move learning forward.

Why? We want teams to be informed about what is most likely to work.

Researching Practices

There are several ways that teachers can uncover evidenced-based recommendations for their colleagues (e.g., Hattie, 2012; Marzano, 2007). One is through the U.S. Department of Education's What Works Clearinghouse (ies.ed.gov/ncee/wwc). This free repository highlights approaches that are documented to be effective. For example, a group of teachers were trying to figure out how to support the learning of their students by mobilizing peers. They found several studies in the What Works Clearinghouse focused on peer-assisted learning strategies and decided to read up on those so that they could create a pilot program to try out tutoring.

> The U.S. Department of Education's What Works Clearinghouse (ies.ed.gov/ncee/wwc) is a free repository that highlights approaches that are documented to be effective.

Sometimes teachers use a specific study or even a personal experience as evidence. That's less powerful, potentially, than using a collection of evidence, but as long as the group agrees to monitor the impact and the implementation of the action, the PLC+ team is doing its work. The reminder is simply not to rely on a single anecdote as the basis of evidence for determining the PLC+ team's next set of actions. As an example, the third-grade teachers at Marshall Elementary School were focused on reading. Their common challenge was that the majority of students were word callers, meaning that they could generally decode the words on a page but had no idea what the sentences meant. The teachers believed that this was the result of a significant push on reading rate in the primary grades and, as one teacher said, "Our students can read fast now. They score in the 90th percentile in oral reading fluency, but they don't always understand what they read. Now we need to slow them down a bit and focus on meaning." They visited each other's classrooms to observe the reading block and met to talk about the strategies they saw in common and where there were differences. (We will spend more time on classroom visits and walk-throughs later in this chapter.)

The Marshall team noted that teachers modeled reading on a regular basis, that students read independently, and that there was a focus in classrooms on vocabulary. They also noted that in five of six classrooms, students were tasked with round robin reading: One student at a time was asked to read a paragraph aloud to the rest of the class. The activator, Mark Hoyt, asked the teacher who did not use round robin to talk about her instructional approach.

She said, "I just don't like seeing some of the students' faces when I call on them to read out loud. They look terrified. I see them counting ahead to figure out which paragraph they will have to read and not really paying attention to the text. But I guess that if everyone is doing it, I should do it too. I don't want my students left out."

Mr. Hoyt responded, "I think we need to investigate this a bit further. How about we all find some expert opinions on this and we meet again on Thursday? I'll email you all what I find, and let's talk about the use of our time for literacy learning." The collaborative team meeting continued, but the conversation focused on what they had learned that day.

On Thursday the group met again. Mr. Hoyt started by saying, "Wow, I was surprised. I couldn't find even one study that said round robin reading was useful. What did you all think about the resources that I sent?" The conversation was animated. To a person, they were surprised by the information. Hazel Washington said, "I read through your information, but then I decided to look for myself. I just couldn't believe that something I've done for years was considered bad practice. I think we need to try something else and see if our kids start to learn to comprehend the text better."

> Teachers visited each other's classrooms to observe the reading block and met to talk about the strategies they saw in common and where there were differences.

The conversation continued, and teachers shared their ideas for replacing round robin reading. They agreed to try a few different things and then readminister the benchmark assessment to see if there was a change in student learning. That would not have happened had the PLC+ been limited to discussing curriculum and assessment issues. Nor would it have happened without facilitation. Including discussions about instruction, and the impact that teaching has on learning, provides an opportunity for teachers to learn and to change their practices.

Another means for finding evidence-based teaching is through the Visible Learning database. John Hattie has created the largest educational research database in history (https://visible-learning.org/hattie-ranking-influences-effect-sizes-learning-achievement). His list includes over 250 influences on learning organized by effect size, or the order of magnitude by which each specific strategy increases students' learning. Larger effect sizes are better, but the choices teachers make should generally be above the average impact of 0.40. Teachers can use Hattie's resource to identify promising practices that they can monitor for impact. But we offer a caution: Don't just pick a strategy without developing the knowledge and skill required to change practice. We can't overemphasize this. Far too often, an instructional strategy is identified but there is no plan in place to develop the knowledge and skills to implement it.

Teams need to identify the essential elements of each strategy they have selected. Opfer and Pedder (2011) argued that teachers need to have complex understandings of teaching or learning before adopting actions and strategies. Without identifying the specific reasons students aren't comprehending, teachers are operating in the dark and will likely pick strategies that may not address the underlying cause of the problem.

The history teachers at Emerson Middle School wanted to address their students' comprehension skills. Their common challenge was that students did not routinely mobilize cognitive strategies such as questioning or summarizing while reading informational texts. It seemed to the teachers that students believed that some people just "got it" and others didn't. As one of the students who was interviewed by the teachers in advance of a collaborative team meeting said, "Either you get it or you don't. It just happens that way."

These history teachers wanted to change that. Using the Hattie database, they discovered reciprocal teaching and the jigsaw method. As

> Including discussions about instruction, and the impact that teaching has on learning, provides an opportunity for teachers to learn and to change their practices.

Sherry Goldberg said, "I've never heard about reciprocal teaching before. It seems like reciprocal teaching could work, because students only read part of a text, and then they practice four comprehension strategies. I'd like to give it a try, and I'd love it if some of you did as well so that we could compare notes about how it's working and if we're doing it right. I know we teach different things, but I think it could be powerful to see if this works."

Reciprocal teaching is a reading comprehension protocol designed by Palincsar and Brown (1984) to assist students in understanding complex texts. It is straightforward enough: Four students read and discuss a text, interacting with peers using strategies that mirror the internal ones used by comprehending readers. The text is segmented into three to five shorter passages so that students periodically pause to discuss what they know thus far and what they find confusing. Students are initially assigned specific roles, which are phased out as students become more adept at text discussion. The roles are these:

- A *summarizer* who assists the group in identifying the key points of the passage

- A *clarifier* who invites questions about confusing vocabulary or concepts

- A *questioner* who poses questions to confirm understanding

- A *predictor* who encourages speculation about information the next passage might reveal

After a few minutes, the team agreed to implement reciprocal teaching and determine the impact that this had on students' comprehension of informational texts. But instruction is not the only thing that team members need to discuss. And, as a reminder, we're not advocating that PLC+ teams just talk about teaching strategies, but rather that they share ideas for tools that have the potential to impact students' learning *and* they actually monitor the impact of their choices. Beyond instructional decisions, teams can discuss the tasks and assignments that they give students. This is an important consideration, as low-level tasks compromise equity efforts and there is evidence that students are not consistently provided with grade-level-appropriate tasks, activities, and assignments that allow them to practice, and then master, content standards.

Low-level tasks compromise equity efforts, and there is evidence that students are not consistently provided with grade-level-appropriate tasks, activities, and assignments that allow them to practice, and then master, content standards.

ASSIGNMENT ANALYSIS

Only by digging in and analyzing assignments can we uncover whether we are appropriately challenging our students. The Education Trust (2016, 2018) has conducted studies of more than 4,000 assignments in English language arts, science, social studies, and math over the last several years to see how teachers are utilizing newer standards in their work. In their words,

> As an equity-focused organization, we are always troubled when assignments in high-poverty schools are less rigorous than those in low-poverty schools. Yes, low expectations take many forms, but classroom assignments are perhaps the most concrete manifestation of them all. (2018, p. 3)

Their analysis of these assignments from high-poverty schools found that the cognitive rigor of many assignments is lacking:

- Assignments were more than twice as likely to focus on procedural skills and fluency (87 percent) compared with conceptual understanding (38 percent) or application of a mathematical concept (39 percent).

- High levels of cognitive demand, defined on Webb's Depth of Knowledge as Level 4, were evident in only 9 percent of math assignments and 5 percent of literacy-based assignments (Webb, 2005).

- Choice and relevance were absent in nearly all the assignments analyzed, with only 2 to 3 percent offering either.

The mathematics team at Atlantic Middle School read the Education Trust reports and recognized that an assignment analysis audit would be beneficial to their overall PLC+ work. "We wondered about how our assignments would hold up," said Zara Singh, a seventh-grade prealgebra teacher. The team first worked through lessons profiled in the report and studied the analysis framework in order to reconceive an assignment on their own. Using the guiding questions published by Education Trust, they scrutinized an assignment of their choice in six categories:

- Alignment to state standards
- Cognitive challenge

- Aspects of rigor (conceptual understanding, procedural skills and understanding, and application)
- Communicating mathematical understanding (constructing and responding to arguments, justifying conclusions)
- Motivation and engagement (relevance)
- Scaffolding

As the activator and department chair, Ms. Singh volunteered to go first when the team met to conduct their assignment analyses. Her willingness to share first demonstrated her vulnerability and built both

PAIR TEACHING STRATEGIES WITH EVIDENCE GATHERING

Teaching strategies abound, but not all have a strong research base behind them. As one example, the practice of teaching to "learning styles" (visual, auditory, and kinesthetic) has no research base, yet remains popular in some quarters (Pasquinelli, 2012). Teachers need comprehensive resources that report on the effectiveness of strategies, so they can make evidence-informed instructional responses about what, when, and with whom to use approaches. Two such comprehensive resources that are easily accessible are John Hattie's Visible Learning research and the U.S. Department of Education's What Works Clearinghouse (https://ies.ed.gov/ncee/wwc).

Consider the common challenge your team has identified. What research-based instructional strategies might be well suited for this purpose? Once the PLC+ has agreed upon a few universal strategies to try, discuss the evidence-gathering method you will use as well to monitor your impact on student learning. Although your team need not be completely lock step in instruction, you will want to agree upon some universal evidence-gathering methods to support a collaborative analysis of the impact of your instructional decisions, and to formatively assess in order to make timely instructional adjustments.

As an example, recall the third-grade team who analyzed a standard and developed learning progressions, learning intentions, and success criteria in Module 5. They identified a common challenge and worked through identifying instructional responses and corresponding evidence-gathering methods to monitor implementation and gauge impact. Importantly, this conversation provided the team with the opportunity to adjust instruction before the end of the unit. Keep in mind that assessment is assessment. Whether it is to be used formatively (e.g., to make instructional adjustments) is a measure of the sophistication of a team. To relegate assessment to a summative function only (e.g., awarding grades) is a lost opportunity. In agreeing on the evidence they would gather and analyze, this third-grade team made it possible to formatively assess and adjust instruction.

NOTES

_____
_____
_____
_____
_____
_____

COLLABORATIVE WORK WITH YOUR TEAM

Module 10:
Pair Teaching Strategies
With Evidence Gathering

page 78 in
The PLC+ Playbook

COACHING CORNERS PROTOCOL

Suggested Time: 20–30 minutes

Purpose: Research-based evidence about instructional strategies is coupled with the expertise within the team. However, knowledge may be distributed differently across the team. Coaching is provided to a small group of colleagues before implementation. Anyone on the team can be a coach; years of experience and expertise are not one and the same. Team members demonstrating a strategy or technique are always volunteers. Use coaching corners to demonstrate and teach a specific strategy or technique to your team. Use the protocol below to build one another's pedagogical content knowledge.

Materials: The activator for Coaching Corners should gather or delegate the gathering of materials for demonstrating the strategies or techniques.

Step 1: Introduce the strategy or technique: Provide background information about the approach, justification/evidence of effectiveness (both personally and in the research base), and any relevant data.

Step 2: Outline the strategy: Consistently using a new practice requires developing specific knowledge, skills, and dispositions. The activator could add the following questions to deepen the learning:

- How is this strategy different than what we are already doing?
- What is about this strategy that leads us to believe it will facilitate learning?
- What is essential to understand about this strategy to implement it?
- What are the basic steps?
- How do you implement it?
- In what context will it be used? (e.g., when introducing content, during small group instruction)
- What are the pitfalls to avoid?

Step 3: Practice session: Lead peers through the identified strategy, or use a short video of yourself implementing it with students. Provide materials used with students, and give time for participants to rehearse the strategy. The practice session should be no more than 10 minutes in length.

Step 4: Feedback and clarifying questions: The "coach" for the session and the "students" provide feedback about the strategy that is helpful, positive, and specific. The discussion should include opportunities to ask and respond to clarifying questions. In addition, discuss opportunities to observe one another enacting the identified instructional strategy.

COLLABORATIVE WORK WITH YOUR TEAM

Module 10:
Coaching Corners Protocol

page 81 in
The PLC+ Playbook

relational trust and collective efficacy. She shared with them the original version of the assignment she chose, and spoke about the gaps she noticed. "I definitely saw that I didn't have any relevance embedded, and there were no choices offered for how students might proceed," she said. But, for her, the most glaring omission had to do with the rigor. "I saw that this assignment could easily be increased in rigor if I moved it from problem sets with the necessary operations identified to requiring students to make decisions about which applications they would need to use," she said. "Now I need your help. What other places could I redesign this assignment to strengthen it?" With that, the team got to work.

In doing so, they built their collective efficacy and came closer to realizing their equity goals. They also noted the different expectations they had for students. Because the activator, who is also the department chair and a well-respected teacher, demonstrated her vulnerability and trust for the team, each of them was more likely to do the same. Over time, the assignments improved, as did student learning. In fact, Atlantic Middle School was recognized as a "school to watch" based on its rising achievement scores.

Assignment analysis is an important tool in creating equitable schools that hold high expectations for all students. Having said that, there are students in every classroom who will struggle to meet the demands of the grade-level standards. Thus, teams spend time focused on compensatory and adaptive approaches to ensure that all students are provided opportunities to learn and the scaffolds necessary for them to learn.

ASSIGNMENT ANALYSIS TOOL

Step 1: Determine the Key Features of the Assignment

Text Type (literary, informational, visual, multiple texts)

Text Length (excerpt, chapter, etc.)

Text Complexity (quantitative and qualitative values that suggest the grade range of the selected text)

Writing Output (no writing, note taking, one or two sentences, multiple short responses, one paragraph, multiple paragraphs)

Length of Assignment (15 minutes or less, one or two class periods, multiple weeks, linked to an ongoing project [quarter/semester/year])

Student Thinking

Webb's *Depth of Knowledge*

• Recall and reproduction
• Basic application of skills/concepts
• Strategic thinking
• Extended thinking

Step 2: Assignment Analysis

1. **Alignment With Standards**

A standards-aligned assignment has essential features. First and most important, it must be grade-level appropriate. The assignment must embrace instructional shifts, including regular practice with complex texts; academic language; read, write, and speak using evidence; and build knowledge through content information. The assignment is clearly articulated so that students can fully understand what is expected of them.

Assignment Analysis for Alignment With Standards

COLLABORATIVE WORK WITH YOUR TEAM

Module 11:
Assignment Analysis Tool
page 84 in
The PLC+ Playbook

COMPENSATORY AND ADAPTIVE APPROACHES

By compensatory supports, we mean additional supports designed to close gaps in learning. Peer tutoring and differentiated instruction are two examples of compensatory supports that we can establish in a classroom. Adaptive systems are those accommodations and modifications needed for students with disabilities to ensure full participation in a general education curriculum. Figure 4.1 includes a comparison of common accommodations and modifications that are useful as teams strive to support all learners.

FIGURE 4.1　Comparing and Contrasting Accommodations and Modifications

Accommodation or Modification	Example
Size: Lowering the number of items a student completes, with no change to difficulty.	• Reducing the number of assigned multiplication problems from 20 to 10, but the difficulty of the problems is not altered. • Reducing the number of chapter review questions from 25 to 15, selecting key questions that assess understanding.
Time: Changing the time you allot for learning, task completion, or testing.	• Providing extra time to complete a test. • Developing a timeline and checklist for completing an extended project with regular check-ins from an adult.
Input: Changing the way instruction is delivered to the learner.	• Having a student listen to a recording of a book after reading the section in a book club. • Giving a student note pages in earth science.
Output: Adapting how the learner can respond to instruction.	• Having a student create a poster instead of a research paper for world history. • Having a student dictate answers for an addition facts worksheet.
Level of support: Changing the amount of personal assistance to an individual learner.	• Recording a conversation with a teacher for later use in writing using a LiveScribe pen. • Having a peer aid a student in constructing a diorama of the first Thanksgiving.
Same only less: Reducing the number of items to change the level of difficulty.	• Reducing the number of possible answers on a multiple-choice quiz from five to two. • Reducing a timed fluency measure to meet the developmental needs of the learner. • Selecting a book at a lower reading level for the student.

Accommodation or Modification	Example
Streamline: Reducing the breadth or focus of an assignment to emphasize the key points.	• Having a student create a list of main points in English instead of writing an essay. • Simplifying vocabulary for a social studies unit of study on explorers.
Same activity with infused objective: IEP objectives or skills are emphasized.	• Phrasing questions so that a student can use his or her eyes to locate the answers *yes* or *no* on a lap tray. • Practicing how to measure in each science lab. • Practicing sight words with peers as part of a "read the room" activity.
Curriculum overlapping: The assignment for one class may be completed in another, and is a replacement.	• A student works on a poster for social studies and receives a grade in language arts as well. • A science lab report is used as a report of information to replace a writing assignment.

Compensatory Supports

The use of initial assessments to identify knowledge and skills gaps (Chapter 3) is also a launching point for PLC+ teams to focus their attention on developing compensatory supports, some of which can be delivered inside the classroom. Peer tutoring, which allows for students to deliver supports to one another, has been reported by Hattie as having an effect size of 0.53, well above the 0.40 effect size associated with one year's worth of growth. For example, Susana Guerrero, a member of the fourth-grade PLC+ at Jefferson Elementary School, learned about dyad reading, a form of peer tutoring that pairs a stronger reader with a weaker one, at a summer university conference she attended. When she returned to school in August, she shared the information with members of her learning community, who agreed that it was worth implementing in their classrooms as a compensatory measure. The technique is deceptively simple. For 15 minutes a day, pairs of students read together aloud from a single book (Brown, Mohr, Wilcox, & Barre, 2016, p. 545):

- Share one book

- Sit side by side

- Track with one smooth finger

- Eyes on words

- Two voices

- Not too fast, not too slow

- Write down crazy words

- Have fun!

The factor that was revolutionary for her, Ms. Guerrero explained to her colleagues, was the text being used. Brown et al. (2016) reported that when the text was two to four grade levels above the current reading level of the assisted reader, students made significant gains on measures of reading comprehension and fluency. "And these were results reported after 90 days," Ms. Guerrero added. Tori Maldonado, another fourth-grade teacher, said, "You know, I've been doing paired reading with my students, but the text was always at the weaker reader's current instructional level. I'd be interested to track this with my kids to see what happens."

When the text was two to four grade levels above the current reading level of the assisted reader, students made significant gains on measures of reading comprehension and fluency.

The PLC+ crafted a plan to implement this compensatory support, beginning with examining the current reading data of their students, assigning pairings, and making decisions about how and when to roll this out across the grade level. They also monitored their results and looked at the interim reading data collected at the 45-day mark. Encouraged by the results they were seeing, the PLC+ decided to continue this compensatory support. By the winter break, the members of the PLC+ were sold on the effectiveness and its ease of use. They met with the principal to share results, noting that the intervention added no additional cost. At the principal's encouragement, the fourth-grade PLC+ met with their colleagues in the third and fifth grades, who were also intrigued.

Differentiated instruction is another avenue for creating compensatory supports. Pioneered by Tomlinson (2001), this approach examines three elements of learning: content, process, and product. While the essential learning is held constant, the means for presenting and assessing can be altered to meet the needs of students. The English teachers working together in the PLC+ at Adams County Middle School focused on implementing differentiated instruction in their classrooms. Their current common challenge was in differentiating instruction through writing processes. The team reached agreements about finding ways to increase conferencing in their classrooms in order to assist writers in developing their skills. *"Scribendo disces scriber,"* said seventh-grade teacher Keith O'Shea. "You learn to write by writing. But we know it's more than just causing writing. They need feedback from us to develop a writer's eye for being able to analyze their own writing."

The team repurposed their existing writing rubrics to develop single-point rubrics to confer with individual students. A single-point rubric isolates the "proficient" column on a rubric. It invites analysis by the student to use evidence to determine where growth is still needed and where expectations have been met or exceeded (see Figure 4.2). India Jackson, another teacher in the PLC+, reported on progress in her class. "I've been using for about two weeks now the single-point writing rubric for argumentation that we wrote, so it's early," she said. "But I've had some promising conversations with students about their writing. I think the best thing so far is that it's requiring them to look more closely at their own writing." Mr. O'Shea nodded his head in agreement. "I've already noticed that I'm getting fewer questions like 'Is this okay?' They know I'm going to turn it back to them to analyze first, before we meet."

Adaptive Supports

In addition to compensatory supports that bridge learning gaps, a smaller number of students require adaptive supports that serve to accommodate or modify learning expectations. Students with disabilities have accommodations and modification articulated within the individualized education program (IEP) or Section 504 plan, which is tailored to the individual needs of the student. These IEPs or 504s are jointly written by a committee composed of the student and family, special educators, and general educators. Accommodations don't substantially change the learning outcomes for students, but instead are designed to improve access. Accommodations can include changes to testing and assessment materials, access to assistive and adaptive technology, adaptations in the physical environment or in how information is presented, and alterations to timing and scheduling for the benefit of the child's learning. Modifications are more significant

FIGURE 4.2   Single-Point Writing Rubric for Middle School

Areas That Need Work	Success Criteria	Evidence of Exceeding Standards
	Topic introduced effectively	
	Related ideas grouped together to give some organization	
	Topic developed with multiple facts, definitions, details	
	Linking words and phrases connect ideas within a category of information	
	Strong concluding statement or section	
	Sentences have clear and complete structure, with appropriate range and variety	
	Knowledge of writing language and conventions shown	
	Any errors in usage do not interfere with meaning	

adaptations and involve decisions that alter the learning expectations for students. Modifications are reserved for students with more significant disabilities. The majority of students with disabilities receive accommodations; comparatively few receive modifications. Therefore, accommodations are about "the how"—how a student receives knowledge and demonstrates mastery. Modifications are about "the what"—what knowledge a student is responsible for learning, and what knowledge he or she will not be learning at this time (Fisher & Frey, 2004).

Members of a PLC+ team at Verona Heights High School had identified communication with general education teachers as a common challenge they faced. At this completely inclusive school, the role of the special educators had changed significantly in the last decade, and thus the PLC+ collaborative teams included both special education teachers and general education teachers in the content area team meetings. In many cases, the English language development specialist participated in the PLC+ collaborative team meetings. No longer were special education students being taught in self-contained classrooms, isolating them and their teachers from the school milieu.

"This was an equity issue," said Janice Baker. "We recognized as a staff that these segregated classrooms resulted in marginalized students who couldn't fully benefit from life at a high school." Over a period of a few years, the school faculty systematically closed self-contained classrooms and redeployed special education personnel in general education classrooms. Now each serves as a member of a content PLC+.

"It's given us a chance to become much better equipped to support the students we have on our caseload in demanding courses like chemistry, British lit, geometry, and government," offered Paul Novak, the special educator who supports the science PLC+ at the school.

However, communication between general and special educators remained a challenge. In the last quarter of the previous school year, members collected and analyzed interview and survey data completed by their general education colleagues. Using this information, they developed new communication tools. "The feedback we got was loud and clear—they wanted information on the first day of school about students with disabilities on their rosters, so they could do a better job creating a welcoming place for all students to be successful. One of the tools they developed together was a digital student profile that they shared with general educators. These profiles are constructed by the special education teacher, who serves as the advocate for the student (i.e., overseeing IEP development, triannual assessments, and such) and is tethered electronically to the student's schedule and teacher's roster (see Figure 4.3). "These profiles don't replace the need for the general education teacher to read the IEP," said Ms. Baker. "But they provide a quick overview so that teachers can gain a sense of goals, accommodations, and other key info

> In addition to compensatory supports that bridge learning gaps, a smaller number of students require adaptive supports that serve to accommodate or modify learning expectations.

FIGURE 4.3 Student Profile Form

CONFIDENTIAL STUDENT PROFILE

This document is used to summarize useful information about a student with an IEP. This does not replace the requirement for all teachers to read the IEP. Please remember this information is confidential.

Student Name: Grade:

Inclusion Specialist: Date:

Areas of strength/interest
- **Aspirations:**

- **Reading:**

- **Writing:**

- **Math:**

- **Social/Emotional:**

- **Behavior:**

IEP goal areas addressed
-

-

Successful learning strategies/adaptations needed
-

Communication strategies/language development needs
- **Strengths:**

- **Needs:**

Positive behavioral support strategies/citizenship supports
- **Strengths:**

- **Needs:**

Important family/health information
-

Additional services that student may need throughout the school day
-

pertaining to the student." The special education PLC+ will be gathering feedback at the end of the first quarter to see if these profiles have been useful, and how they might be improved. "What we want to reduce is the 'on-the-fly' accommodations developed on the day of an assignment or test," said Mr. Novak. "I think we agree that everyone does better when there's a chance to develop accommodations thoughtfully and purposefully."

MOVING TEACHER LEARNING FORWARD

Thus far, this chapter has focused on moving learning forward through intentionally selected instructional practices. In each discussion of instructional approaches, we have noted that teachers need to understand these moves deeply and not just on the surface. "Effective designs for professional learning assist educators in moving beyond comprehension of the surface features of a new idea or practice to developing a more complete understanding of its purposes, critical attributes, meaning, and connection to other approaches" (Learning Forward, 2017). A one-shot professional development event is unlikely to create the deep learning needed to realize the potential, and see the impact, that these strategies can have.

Sustained professional learning, the type that can occur as teams collaborate, is much more likely to create change. As Learning Forward (2017), the world's premiere teacher professional learning membership group, notes, "When educators' knowledge, skills, and dispositions change, they have a broader repertoire of effective strategies to use to adapt their practices to meet performance expectations and student learning needs." There are many forms of effective professional learning for teachers, including these:

- Dialogue with colleagues in which ideas are shared and debated

- Reflective writing in which teachers consider the impact of their decisions

- Peer coaching in which teachers observe one another for impact on learning

- Demonstration lessons in which a small group of teachers observes a peer modeling

- Inquiry with colleagues around a problem or challenge

- Feedback from others focused on a specific area of growth identified by the teacher

- Lesson study and other forms of lesson co-construction in which teachers design, deliver, and evaluate the impact of their instruction

In this chapter, we highlight two additional forms of professional learning, namely learning walks and microteaching. As part of the overall PLC+ framework, we believe that teachers need to deprivatize their practice, open their doors, and visit others. But the point of the visit is to see learning in action. Too many times, visitors to classrooms focus only on the teaching and not the learning. Yes, we believe that there is a relationship between teaching and learning, but when the focus of the visit is only on teaching, there might not be evidence that learning occurred. In addition to learning walks, microteaching or video analysis of small segments of instruction can be a powerful way for teams to magnify and multiply effective practices across the school, again provided that the focus includes learning and not just teaching.

> Too many times, visitors to classrooms focus only on the teaching and not the learning.

LEARNING WALKS

Time is precious for every classroom teacher, and finding the time to spend in each other's classrooms can be a challenge. Yet isolating oneself professionally comes at a much higher cost—a "pathway to burnout" (Schlichte, Yssel, & Merbler, 2005, p. 35). Teaching has long been described as isolating, and the adults in the classroom spend a comparatively low portion of their day in the company of peers. This can chip away at feelings of self-efficacy, not to mention collective efficacy. An important hallmark of successful professional learning communities is that members carve out time to spend with one another in classrooms. Keep in mind that PLC+ teams are *not* groups that meet only on early release days. The heartbeat of a PLC+

rests in the quality time members invest in one another engaged in inquiry of their practices. Time spent in each other's classrooms is an essential part of this equation.

Learning walks are an effective method for exploring common challenges identified by a PLC+. Learning walks differ from instructional rounds (City, Elmore, Fiarman, & Teitel, 2009) in their scope and their formality. Unlike instructional rounds, which use protocols for establishing long-term networks, defining problems of practice, and formally analyzing patterns, learning walks are more loosely structured. As with the use of video for professional learning, these "walks" require professional learning and practice. For example, those teachers engaging in learning walks must learn to discern between descriptive and evaluative statements. Also, learning walks are *most effective* when focused on specific problems of practice (POP). In some cases, the host teacher determines the POP. In others, it is jointly determined by the PLC+.

Ghost Walks

Visiting empty classrooms is a great way to conduct a learning walk, especially for PLC+ teams that have not conducted learning walks before. PLC+ members make their classrooms available during a prep period and in turn are participants in the ghost walk, where the observation is confined to discussion about the physical environment. Baldwin Elementary School was focused on getting better at communicating learning intentions and success criteria to students. Teachers in the primary grades PLC+ used a ghost walk to see how their colleagues accomplished this with emergent readers.

Capacity-Building Learning Walk

Some learning walks are conducted expressly for the purpose of gathering evidence to inform decisions. A PLC+ team at Baldwin Elementary uses capacity-building learning walks with faculty who are new to their school. PLC+ colleagues are paired with the new teachers so that they can discuss how PLC+ efforts are evidenced in classrooms. Ms. Salisbury accompanied first-grade teacher Xavier Dias on a capacity-building learning walk focused on teacher modeling of expert thinking.

"Mr. Dias wasn't really familiar with teacher modeling when he arrived here at Baldwin," explained Ms. Salisbury. "So we went to three classrooms during rotations, when our students were at art or P.E.," she said. "It was prearranged, and he got to see three teachers doing a think-aloud to model their expert thinking in real time," she said.

Mr. Dias added, "It helped me tremendously. I've read transcripts of think-alouds, but seeing the interactions between teacher and students gave me a better sense of it. I'll be trying it out tomorrow."

The third- and fifth-grade teachers at Red Canyon Elementary School conducted a capacity-building learning walk with Tori Maldonado, a member of the fourth-grade PLC+, to learn more about the logistics of dyad reading. The third- and fifth-grade teachers were energized by the findings shared by their fourth-grade colleagues on pairing readers to jointly read more complex texts, but they still had questions regarding implementation. "It's actually simpler than I imagined," said one third-grade teacher, "and it was helpful to talk with a few students about their impressions."

Faculty Learning Walks

Ideally, each teacher participates in two each year. In many cases, this can be achieved by coordinating planning periods so that coverage is not an issue. Teachers are therefore grouped by convenience, but this in itself can create interesting conversations among teachers who don't otherwise have much contact with one another. Teachers often come away with ways to innovate in their own classrooms, and even to form new partnerships. A series of learning walks concerning the practice of close reading of complex texts resulted in an interdisciplinary lesson between science and English teachers. Students read and discussed a passage written by Charles Darwin twice in a two-day span. Their English teacher used the passage to discuss how the author of *The Origin of Species* used claim, evidence, and reasoning to forward a theory of evolution. Their biology teacher focused on the content of the passage and its connection to a groundbreaking insight that changed the life sciences. (See Figure 4.4 for a summary of these learning walks.)

FIGURE 4.4   Types of Learning Walks

Type of Walk	Purpose	Recommended Time	Participants	Follow-Up After the Walk
Ghost Walk	This walk is to examine classrooms without students present. Teachers volunteer to make their classrooms available, and in turn are participants in the ghost walk. The focus of the observation is about the physical learning environment.	1 hour	Principal, assistant principal, teachers, building leadership team, coaches, professional learning community.	Summary of data collected: evidence and wonderings processed with entire faculty.
Capacity-Building Learning Walks	This walk focuses solely on collecting data to inform decisions. Collection of data and evidence helps identify the implementation of effective practices and gain insights into next steps.	1 hour	Principal, assistant principal, coaches, and other members of the building's leadership team.	Summary of data collected: evidence and wonderings processed with entire faculty.
Faculty Learning Walks	The goal of this learning walk is to focus on the learning of the whole staff. It involves all teachers in visiting other teachers' classrooms outside of the PLC+ to which members belong. This can spark new ideas and strategies for teachers to incorporate into their own practice.	All day	Principal, assistant principal, and whoever is available each period and/or time segment, ultimately involving entire faculty throughout the year.	Summary of data collected: evidence and wonderings processed with entire faculty.

Learning walks are best conducted with some boundaries in mind, lest they devolve into the kind of judgmental discourse many teachers fear. Participation is always voluntary, and teachers who open their classrooms to such visits always receive advance notice. Visitors meet in advance with a facilitator from their professional learning community who revisits expectations and purpose and who reminds PLC+ members to refrain from taking notes, as it can raise anxiety levels. We take steps to ensure that the teachers whose classrooms are visited get opportunities to serve as members of a learning walk team as well, no matter how well acquainted faculty are with the learning walks or walk-through process.

After spending a short time in each classroom (no more than 15 minutes, and often less), they meet again to engage in a reflective conversation led by the activator. They are asked what they noticed, what was surprising, and what was held in common with their own practice. The activator moderates so that the conversation doesn't become evaluative and stays focused on the learning of the teachers. Importantly, this reflective conversation must end with teachers sharing insights they have made about their own classrooms. Time is reserved at the next PLC+ gathering for observers and host teachers to share their impressions with one another.

Video must serve as fodder for the discussion a teacher has with another, encouraging the teacher to notice the moves he or she is making as well as the impact those moves have on student learning.

The quest for better learning should not be limited to instructional strategies and tools that teachers can implement. Rather, peers, coaches, and administrators can use microteaching to foster honest and reflective conversations. We did not say that these conversations would be easy. In fact, our colleague Jennifer Abrams (2016) notes that they are often hard conversations. But evidence-based conversations can be consequential, impacting both the teachers' teaching and the students' learning.

USING MICROTEACHING TO IMPROVE TEACHING AND LEARNING

We believe that the day is coming in which microteaching, using clips of video to discuss the learning experience with a colleague, will be commonplace (Shaw, 2017).

CAPACITY-BUILDING LEARNING WALK

Suggested Time: 2 hours

Purpose: To collect observational data about an agreed-upon focus, in order to assist our PLC+ team in gaining insight into implementation, and to make decisions about our next steps.

Focus: We are examining _____

SCHEDULE (No more than 7 minutes per class)	WHAT IS THE TEACHER DOING? Team A	HOW DO STUDENTS DESCRIBE THEIR LEARNING? Team B	HOW DOES THE ENVIRONMENT SUPPORT THE LEARNING? Team C
Classroom 1: Time:			
Classroom 2: Time:			
Classroom 3: Time:			

ROUND 1 DEBRIEF OF CLASSROOMS 1–3: WHAT PATTERNS DID WE NOTICE IN EACH OF THESE THREE AREAS?

SCHEDULE (No more than 7 minutes per class)	WHAT IS THE TEACHER DOING? Team B	HOW DO STUDENTS DESCRIBE THEIR LEARNING? Team C	HOW DOES THE ENVIRONMENT SUPPORT THE LEARNING? Team A
Classroom 4: Time:			
Classroom 5: Time:			

CAPACITY-BUILDING LEARNING WALK DEBRIEFING NOTES

Focus: We are examining _____

ROUND 1 DEBRIEF: PATTERNED OBSERVATIONS OF TEAMS A, B, AND C (9 minutes)

Team A reports on what the teachers were doing.	Team B reports on how students described their learning.	Team C reports on the ways in which the environment supported the learning.

ROUND 2 DEBRIEF: PATTERNED OBSERVATIONS OF TEAMS B, C, AND A (9 minutes)

Team B reports on what the teachers were doing.	Team C reports on how students described their learning.	Team A reports on the ways in which the environment supported the learning.

ROUND 3 DEBRIEF: PATTERNED OBSERVATIONS OF TEAMS C, A, AND B (9 minutes)

Team C reports on what the teachers were doing.	Team A reports on how students described their learning.	Team B reports on the ways in which the environment supported the learning.

OVERALL DEBRIEF OF THE EXPERIENCE (20 minutes)

What conclusions can we reach about implementation?

What conclusions can we reach about strengths?

What conclusions can we reach about opportunities for growth as a team?

How might we refine this process for future capacity-building learning walks?

COLLABORATIVE WORK WITH YOUR TEAM

Module 12:
Capacity-Building Learning Walk
page 90 in
The PLC+ Playbook

Module 12:
Capacity-Building Learning Walk Debriefing Notes
page 92 in
The PLC+ Playbook

Module 12:
Team Time Discussion
page 93 in
The PLC+ Playbook

TEAM TIME DISCUSSION

QUESTION	MY THOUGHTS	OUR COLLECTIVE THOUGHTS
What is the value to our collective efforts in conducting learning walks?		
How can learning walks develop our individual and collective efficacy?		
What are some important considerations to think about when considering learning walks to strengthen our team?		
Where might be an entry point for our PLC+ to begin exploring learning walks?		

PREPARATION FOR MICROTEACHING:
THE VOLUNTEER TEACHER

BEFORE FILMING:

What are your goals for this
process (e.g., to improve a teaching
technique, to refine your ability
to engage in expert noticing, to
identify the thinking of a student)?

When and with whom will you need
to schedule filming? Who will you
need for assistance before, during,
or after filming?

What equipment will you need?

What do you hope to capture in
the video? What specifically do you
hope to see from your students?
What aspects of their learning do
you hope will progress and move
forward?

AFTER FILMING:

Schedule time to review the footage.

In what ways was the lesson you
delivered different from the lesson
you planned?

What questions does the video
raise for you? What did you see
from your students that raised
those questions?

(Continued)

COLLABORATIVE WORK WITH YOUR TEAM

Module 13:
Preparation for
Microteaching: The
Volunteer Teacher
page 97 in
The PLC+ Playbook

Importantly, there is strong evidence that microteaching works. In his review of research, Hattie (2012) collected meta-analyses, or statistical compilations of many studies on the same topic (e.g., collective teacher efficacy, formative evaluation of teaching, feedback, goal intentions, success criteria, and microteaching, to name a few). Microteaching has an effect size of 0.88, more than double the average impact of the teaching practices Hattie evaluated. Thus, we believe that it should be more common in schools. But simply video-recording classrooms is not going to result in the impact noted in Hattie's review. Instead, the video must serve as fodder for the discussion a teacher has with another, encouraging the teacher to notice the moves he or she is making as well as the impact those moves have on student learning.

Two members of the math PLC+ at Arrowhead High School, Greg Davidson and Ricardo Furner, have a standing appointment every other week with one another to watch video of one of them teaching. These two members have devoted a significant amount of time to their own professional learning around the use of video to improve their teaching by closely examining and critiquing their instructional moves. The teacher being observed determines what he wants the inquiry conversation to focus upon. During their discussion, Mr. Davidson uses his skills in cognitive coaching and reflective teaching to ensure that he does not tell Mr. Furner what he thinks about the lesson, but rather they co-construct the thinking about the experience. They watch the clip of Mr. Furner teaching together and discuss it.

Mr. Furner said, "Here's the part I wanted you to see. I'm working with a small group of students who are taking on a rich mathematical task. It's that one we developed in our PLC+ two weeks ago. But they got stuck and so did I. Help me figure out what I could have done differently."

Mr. Davidson asks his colleague reflective questions (e.g., "What do you think these students knew and didn't know when they first asked for help?"), and the two of them speculate together about alternative tactics. "It's kind of like looking at game tapes after a football game," said Mr. Davidson. He and Mr. Furner are coaches for the junior varsity flag football team. "We're rerunning plays to see what we might do differently the next time." They ponder the impact of specific moves and note ways that might have resulted in increased learning. Consistent with a microteaching approach, they focus on short segments of the video, dissecting teacher moves and students' responses to those moves. In other words, they do not limit their conversation to teaching; learning is also important.

CONCLUSION

When considering the reply to the question "How do we move learning forward?" teams need to consider the ways to meet the needs of each learner. These conversations focus teams on becoming informed about what is most likely to work. None of us have all of the answers, but together we probably have answers that will work. When teams engage in understanding evidence-based instructional strategies, they are motivated and empowered to address the common challenge that they have for themselves and their students and measure the impact these strategies have on teaching and learning. The process for answering the question "How do we move learning forward?" is summarized here:

- Identifying effective, evidence-based instructional approaches
- Analyzing assignments for rigor
- Developing compensatory and adaptive approaches
- Implementing professional learning through learning walks and microteaching

As teams discuss how to learn moving learning forward, they should keep the four crosscutting values in mind. These ensure that the PLC+ process is delivering on the promise of equity while also ensuring that team members' voices are heard. The following table provides a summary and some reflective questions that pull your PLC+ team back to the crosscutting values to keep in mind as you engage in this aspect of the work.

EQUITY	Equity demands that all students receive relevant and impactful instructional strategies and appropriately aligned tasks and assignments that allow them to practice and master content. Unfortunately, some students do not receive high-quality instruction and fail to achieve as a result.
	• How does your PLC+ come to know all of your students so learning opportunities can make personal connections?
	• Do all students have access to evidence-based instructional approaches?
	• Do teachers and teams monitor the impact of the instruction?
HIGH EXPECTATIONS	If you are going to put the effort into holding your students to high expectations, which will often begin with establishing appropriate learning intentions and success criteria, there also needs to be consideration in determining the success of the instructional decisions of your PLC+.
	• How does your PLC+ measure success?
	• How do you diagnose student learning needs to close gaps for your students?
	• How does your PLC+ determine instructional strategies that will best support students in meeting their learning expectations?
INDIVIDUAL AND COLLECTIVE EFFICACY	Trust is an important part of building efficacy. And being vulnerable and open to learning is important. To build collective efficacy, teachers and teams must learn to determine the impact of instructional decisions on student learning. It requires an honest evaluation of what the teachers did that did or did not move learning forward.
	• What evidence does your PLC+ gather and analyze to determine the impact of their instructional decisions on student learning?
	• What evidence does your PLC+ gather and analyze to determine the implementation of your action?
	• How do you use evidence of student learning to determine the learning needs of your PLC+?
	• Do you visit one another's classrooms and engage in microteaching?

ACTIVATION	As you have seen in this chapter, there are numerous instructional strategies that teachers have access to so that student learning continuously moves forward. It is important to ensure that strategies selected are evidence based and appropriate for the learning needs of your students. Many teachers have strategies that they use without knowledge of the research behind them or the impact they can potentially have on student learning.

- When discussing different strategies in your PLC+ to use in the classroom, what would be an important role of the activator?

- How might the PLC+ facilitate dialogue around the validity of the selection of specific strategies?

- In what ways can the activator ensure that all voices in the PLC+ are heard when thinking about strategies that will move learning forward?

COLLABORATIVE WORK
WITH YOUR TEAM

Module 14:
Equity and
Expectations
Values Checklist

page 100 in
The PLC+ Playbook

EQUITY AND EXPECTATIONS VALUES CHECKLIST

The core values of the PLC+ framework include equity and expectations. Without these values, student learning varies considerably, and often students are blamed for their lack of progress or achievement. Members of a PLC+ team assume responsibility for the learning of all students and are willing to talk honestly, and openly, about how they can best meet the needs of all of their students. When we directly discuss the values of equity and expectations, we may uncover assumptions that need to be addressed. The following checklist provides some questions that PLC+ teams have found useful in checking in on their values.

QUESTION	MY THOUGHTS	OUR COLLECTIVE THOUGHTS
Did we consider the best evidence for the instructional approaches we discussed?		
Did we analyze assignments for their appropriateness?		
Did we provide compensatory and adaptive supports for students who needed them?		
Do we overscaffold for some students because we believe that they cannot achieve at the same level as other students?		
Did we discuss our visits to each other's classrooms with a focus on teaching *and* learning?		
Have we agreed to video-record our instruction and talk with peers about improving both teaching *and* learning?		
Do we have a plan that will allow us to address the common challenge?		

ACTIVATE LEARNING FOR MYSELF AND OTHERS CHECKLIST

Student learning needs drive adult learning needs. Once teams understand where students are now in their learning journey, teams need to take a step back to reflect on their personal learning. Are there any adult learning needs that must be met to best be able to support student learning? As already discussed, the + in the PLC+ is you, and so it is important to recognize learning for teachers is a constant. Given that you want to move student learning forward, what learning do you (or your team) need to accomplish to ensure that all students are successful?

WHAT DID WE DECIDE TO DO TO MOVE STUDENT LEARNING FORWARD?	WHAT ARE MY LEARNING NEEDS SO I CAN MEET MY STUDENTS' LEARNING NEEDS? What strategies might I need to learn more about?	WHAT LEARNING WILL I ENGAGE IN TO MEET MY LEARNING NEEDS? What will I do on my own? What can I do with colleagues?

COLLABORATIVE WORK WITH YOUR TEAM

Module 14:
Activate Learning for Myself and Others Checklist

page 101 in
The PLC+ Playbook

COLLECTIVE EFFICACY CHECKLIST

Teams that are empowered to make decisions, act, communicate clearly, and hold themselves accountable for their efforts manifest high degrees of collective teacher efficacy (CTE). Use the checklist below to gauge and monitor the actions that will follow your work about the third question, "How do we move learning forward?"

QUESTION	MY THOUGHTS	OUR COLLECTIVE THOUGHTS
How confident are we in the evidence used to select instructional strategies?		
What data will we collect that demonstrate success for the team?		
Do we believe we have the skills and knowledge necessary to implement the strategies we have identified?		
Do all of our team members feel supported as they try new strategies and approaches?		

COLLABORATIVE WORK WITH YOUR TEAM

Module 14:
Collective Efficacy Checklist

page 102 in
The PLC+ Playbook

QUESTION 4:

What did we LEARN TODAY?

PLC+ Framework Guiding Questions

1. **Where are we going?**

2. **Where are we now?**

3. **How do we move learning forward?**

4. **What did we learn today?**

5. **Who benefited and who did not benefit?**

THE STORY BEHIND THE QUESTION

This question requires PLC+ collaborative teams to look at evidence of learning, reflect on that aggregated and disaggregated evidence of learning, and then move forward with this evidence in mind. This forward movement could require PLC+ team members to engage in furthering their own professional learning or simply changing their approach to teaching this particular skill or content. Successfully addressing this question will leave the PLC+ laser-focused on who did and did not benefit from instruction—the topic of Chapter 6.

Effective activation and facilitation of this particular question supports engaging in dialogue about those learners that did and did not make learning gains without sliding into excuses and blame. The facilitation of this particular question will lead the group to focus on *impact*. There must be facilitated dialogue around the learning tasks they engineered, the strategies they used to support students in

Video 6
Introduction to Chapter 5

resources.corwin.com/
plcplus

engaging in those tasks, and as a result, how well students performed against the established learning intentions.

With regard to **equity**, this particular question is about outcomes. Did all students learn what they were supposed to learn? If not, why not? Importantly, this question includes the word *today*. For us, this has many meanings. For the individual classroom teacher, the question begs for checking for understanding so that immediate action can be taken if some students did not learn. At the team level, *today* focuses on more aggregate information. The establishment of high **expectations** for student learning is critical. This will oftentimes begin with looking at the skills, concepts, and rigor level within a standard. Yet designing learning tasks that connect to those expectations as well as scoring student work against those expectations are additional layers that need to have a place within your PLC+.

Learning together as a **collective** whole is one way to drive individual and collective efficacy, as we purposefully and intentionally make decisions about which evidence-based practice to use in moving learning forward.

A PLC+ TEAM IN ACTION

David Flynn began his PLC+ collaborative team meeting saying, "What did we learn today?" Over the past several sessions, the team has spent time addressing the three previous questions: "Where are we going?" "Where are we now?" and "How do we move learning forward?" This fourth question is one we typically ask our students, but it's a great question for professional learning community members to ask of themselves, especially around their problem of practice or common challenge. We should be learning about ourselves and our students on a daily basis. And we should reflect on our answers to this question to determine what else we need to do to accomplish our goals.

In response to Mr. Flynn's question, Stacy Murray said, "I learned that our students are very resilient. They had a really complex piece of text to read, and they stuck with it for the whole lesson. I'm feeling really good about it. Did you all have similar experiences?"

Mr. Flynn charted what the team had learned so that they could see future opportunities and celebrate their learning. The team talked for a few minutes about one of their common challenges, which was to increase stamina across the learning environment. They agreed it seemed that student perseverance was increasing, and that it was probably time to measure it again in a more formal way. The use of the word *seemed* is deliberate in this context. Mr. Flynn and his fellow PLC+ team members recognize that their answers to this question are tentative until they look at the data to support or refute the claim.

Mr. Flynn, the activator, then returned to the original question. "What else did we learn today?" To help organize the assertions or answers to this question, Mr. Flynn charted the responses of his fellow PLC+ colleagues. After a short pause, Shawna Little said, "I'm not sure yet what I learned. I'd like to have some time to look at the student work we brought. I'm happy to go first, if people are ready to move to this." They agreed that examining student work was appropriate. Ms. Little presented her students' work and invited team members to comment.

The team turned their attention to the student work products that Ms. Little had provided. The unit of study focused on the Gold Rush, and students had been writing about this period in history. The genre focus was informational writing, and students had drafted research papers. Each member of the team selected three samples of student work and read through them. Using the district's writing rubric, they made notes about individual student needs as well as trends they saw across the papers they reviewed. Members then traded papers with a partner and reviewed those papers as well, again noting individual and collective trends.

For example, Amber Hastings said, "I see lots of details in these papers. They are very descriptive, and their word choice is really strong. But I do notice that they all start the same way. They turn the prompt into a question. The questions are a little different from each other, but it feels kind of formulaic."

Mr. Flynn asked, "What do you all think might explain this behavior? Why do you think that so many students use questions to start their papers?"

Mr. Flynn and his fellow PLC+ team members recognize that their answers to this question are tentative until they look at the data to support or refute the claim.

The members of this team talked about several ideas, including that it's an easy way to start the paper and that they have used this approach successfully in the past. Ms. Hastings added, "I'm thinking about my students and realizing that we taught this tool. We showed them that the use of the question could hook the reader. But they've overgeneralized, or we overtaught. We need to focus on other introduction tools."

Tricia Yarborough added, "I'm seeing pretty much the same trends. I'm really impressed with the vocabulary usage, and I hope we see that across the grade. I'd like to talk more about Anthony when we get a chance. I see a lot of struggle in his paper. Well, actually in his thinking. I'm concerned that he's falling further behind."

This process continued with teachers looking at student work from their own classrooms and those of their peers. We do not recommend that teachers wait six weeks for a team meeting to do this. Rather, looking at student work regularly allows teachers to reflect on and regularly adjust their practice.

To our thinking, focusing on "what we learned today" invites teachers into conversations about students' learning as well. Looking at student work surfaces barriers to student learning (e.g., the assessment itself, the instructional approach/resources, teachers' biases). But in the PLC+ framework, teams are focused on what teachers are learning about themselves and their students as a result of analyzing the work. That's the key—what are we learning that we can use to make a difference? And this is not a once-and-done question. Looking at student work and asking, "What have we learned today?" allows teachers and teams to see whether their practices are having the desired effect on student learning.

In the PLC+ framework, teams are focused on what teachers are learning about themselves and their students as a result of analyzing the work. That's the key—what are we learning that we can use to make a difference?

This question also opens the door for formative assessment processes (e.g., Ainsworth, 2014) as well as more formal protocols for collaborative analysis of student work (Colton, Langer, & Goff, 2015). In addition, this process allows teachers an opportunity to review and discuss the expectations they have for students and whether those expectations are, at a minimum, held in common across the grade or department. We also recognize that teams can visit other schools to refine their expectations as well.

This is exactly what happened in a different collaborative team meeting of this same fourth-grade team. They were focused on mathematics and had administered a common assessment. Mr. Flynn had aggregated the results, and the team was talking about the trends they observed when Amanda Pelzer said, "I want to be honest with you. I think it's my class that is bringing the averages down. This is really complex math. I wasn't sure that it was even appropriate for fourth graders. But I see that a lot of our students did well on this assessment, so I think my expectations were probably off. If I don't think they'll learn it, they won't. I need to go back and review this with them. Dave, can you exclude my class and let us talk about the other students?"

Ms. Pelzer obviously trusted her team and allowed herself to be vulnerable. That's powerful and will likely have an impact on her in the short term and on her students in the long run. We'd also like to note that this experience was only possible because the team had already talked about where they were going, where they are now, and how they could move learning forward. Without answers to those questions, it's unlikely that they would have even had a common assessment, much less talked about it as a team. In part, answering this question requires that teachers understand how to reflect.

REFLECTION

It sounds so easy: "Reflect on the experience." In reality, it's actually more complex. When we reflect, we consider deeply something that we might not otherwise have given much thought to. This helps us to learn. Reflection requires consciously examining and thinking about our experiences, actions, feelings, and responses, and then interpreting or analyzing them in order to learn from them (Atkins & Murphy, 1994; Boud, Cohen, & Sampson, 1999; Boud, Keogh, & Walker, 1985). Typically, we do this by asking ourselves questions about what we did, how we did it, and what we learned about our practice, ourselves, and our students from doing it. Furthermore, this type of thinking can prompt us to consider what we might do differently in both the proximal and distal future, and what led us

True reflection connects our new learning with actions moving forward.

to this particular point in teaching and learning. Reflecting on academic or professional practice in this way may make our personal beliefs, expectations, and biases more evident to us. Horn and Little (2010) noted that talking about student learning was a catalyst for moving teams out of stagnant unproductive dialogue. When teams talked about student learning in a businesslike manner, educators were able to fully examine the impact of implications of their actions on the learning and thinking of their students.

Reflection is more than a summary of what was talked about or discussed. True reflection connects our new learning with actions moving forward. If we simply reflect, but never ignite change as a result of that reflection, we lose the power that genuine and authentic reflection can have. In order to be individually and collectively efficacious, we need to be able to process and articulate our new learning as well as determine what actions this new learning has caused. A simple example may be that in your PLC+, you may have learned that students already bring a wealth of knowledge to the learning experience, which means that everything that is currently taught isn't necessarily always needed. An action connected to this new learning is to devise quick initial assessments for targeted skills and concepts in your upcoming unit to better determine the entry point for instruction that meets the readiness levels of your students.

As John Dewey noted, "We do not learn from experience . . . ; we learn from reflecting on experience."

Below are a series of questions that will support the reflection process in your PLC+:

- What did we focus our PLC+ discussion on today?

- What evidence did we look at, and what did it "tell" us?

- What was affirmed though our PLC+ discussions or analysis?

- What did I learn as a result of the discussion and/or analysis?

- How did this change the way I currently think, or disrupt assumptions I had?

- How can my learning positively impact my students?

- How did this help me determine the impact of my instructional decisions?

- What might I need to learn more about?

- What action(s) will I take as a result of this discussion and/or analysis?

The purpose behind these questions is not to merely discuss one and then move on to the next question, but to promote dialogue among PLC+ team members through active listening, paraphrasing, questioning, and critically examining responses to each question. Megan Andrews asked her team of arts teachers to think about what they learned as a result of their collective analysis of student performances. Some of their answers focused on student learning, such as "Some students have a lot of fear about performing, while others experience great excitement," and "The skill levels of our students vary widely, and we're not really doing anything special for that." Other responses focused on what teachers learned about their own practices, such as "I have not provided students enough practice in front of an audience," and "We have not discussed stage fright and how to deal with the butterflies that are from both fear and excitement."

Ms. Andrews then asked, "How did this change your thinking, or what did you need to learn more about?"

This generated a lot of additional discussion, including the need to teach stress management techniques, schedule skills clinics for specific students, and add practice time on the stage rather than only in the classroom. As one of the teachers commented, "This allowed me to see our expectations from the students' perspective. Many of them were excited, but we need to think about those who need more support either in terms of skill or in terms of confidence and stress. I'd like to see us come back to this for the next collaborative team meeting and develop some concrete plans." The team agreed.

Reflecting is important, as we hope you have seen. As John Dewey noted, "We do not learn from experience . . . ; we learn from reflecting

COLLABORATIVE WORK WITH YOUR TEAM

Module 15:
Team Time Discussion
page 107 in
The PLC+ Playbook

on experience." But team members also need to have experiences on which to reflect. And they need to learn to notice so that they can collect those experiences on which to reflect. In the next section, we'll briefly discuss expert noticing and describe how teams can help each other develop their expert noticing skills.

EXPERT NOTICING

Gibson and Ross (2016) define noticing as "the ways in which teachers are able during instruction to observe important details in students' responses, and interpret this information accurately and comprehensively to adapt instruction in the moment" (p. 181). Novice noticers use a simple binary metric to gauge a student's knowledge—the response is either correct or incorrect, tending to narrow subsequent choices for students to move them to a correct response. However, giving students limited choices reduces their ability to consolidate their thinking, strengthen links to prior learning, and deepen their schema (Choppin, 2011). Without this essential cognitive and metacognitive development, students fail to master higher-order conceptual thinking. You'll recall from previous chapters that limiting access to more rigorous and challenging thinking is ultimately an equity issue that disproportionately impacts students of color, those who live in poverty, English language learners, and students with disabilities (Hwang, Choi, Bae, & Shin, 2018).

Expert noticers, however, are able to ask themselves, "What does this student know and not know at this moment such that he or she gave that incorrect answer?" An expert noticer would also ask what he or she did that elicited the answer. For example, "Did I ask the wrong question?" Unlike the novice, an expert noticer can provide strategically crafted feedback to students, prompting them to consolidate and extend understanding of the topic of study.

> "What does this student know and not know at this moment such that he or she gave that incorrect answer?"

Expert noticing is not necessarily developed through years on the job alone. It needs to be learned. In order to do so, members of the science professional learning community at George Washington Carver High School took on this challenge. They began by observing their colleague Jada Butler. Ms. Butler invited two of her ninth-grade students to attend a PLC+ collaborative team meeting so that they could participate in a fishbowl, where team members observed her teaching an earth science lesson. While her colleagues watched, Ms. Butler, a National Board Certified Teacher, worked with Raevon and Shirlese as they engaged in a series of activities about normal, thrust, and strike-slip faults and their associated boundaries. Using a model designed by the American Geosciences Institute ("A Model of Three Faults," adapted from the USGS Learning Web Lesson Plans, American Geosciences Institute, https://www.earthsciweek .org/classroom-activities/a-model-of-three-faults), she queried her two students about their predictions about which way designated points would move relative to one another, remembering to ask them for justifications.

Addressing her colleagues for a moment, she said, "If I can't hear their logic, I can't get a good idea about how to respond. That's why I ask them a follow-up when they don't tell me why on their own."

She asked them to compare what happened to the rock layers in a thrust fault and a strike-slip fault. When Raevon answered incorrectly, she said, "Tell me more about that. Walk me through your thinking."

As the boy explained his logic, he realized his error and changed his reply. Pausing to speak to her colleagues, Ms. Butler said, "I love when that happens! Sometimes just giving them the opportunity to listen to their own reasoning is enough to catch their own errors and correct them."

When Shirlese had difficulty calculating the scale of the model to correlate it to the magnitude of the 1906 San Francisco earthquake, Ms. Butler asked questions at first. When that was not successful, she moved to more overt prompts, or cognitive nudges and cues, before moving back to doing reteaching. This time, Shirlese was successful. Once more, Ms. Butler turned her attention to her colleagues. "Sometimes prompts and cues aren't sufficient. When I give them a cue to direct their attention to some salient information that could help them, they don't always recognize it. I don't want to fall into the trap

EXPERT NOTICING VIDEO PROTOCOL

Select a short video for use with your team. Be sure that the video chosen has substantial student dialogue that can be easily heard. Videos that are closed-captioned are especially useful.

Step 1: Watch the video in full and without interruption. Then replay it and take notes on the following questions. Discuss these briefly as a team to arrive at consensus.

QUESTION	MY THOUGHTS	OUR COLLECTIVE THOUGHTS
What was the teacher trying to accomplish?		
How would you describe the role(s) of the teacher?		
How would you describe the role(s) of the students?		

Step 2: Student Strengths: Now watch the video a third time, and home in on the thinking of the student(s). Do not become distracted by extraneous information, such as the room décor, miscellaneous student behaviors, and general instructional strategies. First focus on the strengths of the students' thinking, using language frames like those below (Jilk, 2016):

"_____ seemed to summarize learning when she or he said _____."

"_____ seemed to organize her or his thinking when she or he said _____."

"_____ seemed to notice a pattern when she or he said _____."

"_____ seemed to transfer learning when she or he said _____."

"_____ seemed to make a hypothesis when she or he said _____."

"_____ pressed for clarification when she or he said _____."

Use the noticing note-taking guide on page 113 to record your thoughts and those of your team.

COLLABORATIVE WORK WITH YOUR TEAM

Module 16:
Expert Noticing
Video Protocol
page 110 in
The PLC+ Playbook

TEAM TIME DISCUSSION

Expert noticing develops with practice and is best applied in your own classroom. How might you foster your own continued professional learning on expert noticing? What steps might your team take to learn together? Use the discussion questions below to consider steps you and your team will take.

QUESTION	MY THOUGHTS	OUR COLLECTIVE THOUGHTS	COMMITTED ACTIONS
How can the development of expert noticing impact our classroom practice(s)?			
What will I be mindful of as I interact with students?			
How might I use the collective knowledge of my team to improve my expert noticing?			
What human and material resources can we access to further develop our expert noticing skills?			

NOTICING NOTE-TAKING GUIDE

	MY THOUGHTS	OUR COLLECTIVE THOUGHTS
Step 1: Initial viewing of video		
Step 2: Evidence of student learning strengths		
Step 3: Evidence of student errors or misconceptions		
Step 4: Interpretation of student thinking		
Step 5: Recommendations for responses		

COLLABORATIVE WORK WITH YOUR TEAM

Module 16:
Team Time Discussion
page 112 in
The PLC+ Playbook

COLLABORATIVE WORK WITH YOUR TEAM

Module 16:
Noticing Note-Taking Guide
page 113 in
The PLC+ Playbook

of just leading her to say the correct response, with little understanding of why it is so. That's when I go back to doing some review, then start the cycle of questioning again." This is an example of an expert noticer—she asks herself what the learner may be misinterpreting in order to figure out what to do next.

"We can't get better without you in the equation," teacher Marquis Jackson said to the students when the 20-minute fishbowl was over. He then turned back to Ms. Butler. "Jada, I'm going to film myself next week to improve my noticing. Can I schedule a microteaching round with you?"

COMMON ASSESSMENTS AS TRIGGERS FOR REFLECTION

Noticing works as fodder for collective reflecting, especially when members have had similar experiences with students. One of the ways that PLC+ teams can accomplish this is through the use of common assessments. As part of their work, PLC+ team members often design, develop, or modify assessment items that are subsequently administered to all students regardless of what teacher they have. The specific items are developed to provide information that helps teachers determine what students are understanding, where there are gaps in comprehension, and who needs additional support or even intervention. As groups of teachers develop these assessment items, they learn more about the content standards and how those standards might be assessed on summative instruments such as state or national tests. In addition, they plan distractor items on multiple-choice questions such that they know when students overgeneralize, oversimplify, or exhibit common misunderstandings about the content. In some schools, a number of the common formative assessment items mirror the state test design. As Michael Ellis, a science teacher said, "We know that test format practice is critical. Students must understand tests as a genre—how they work and what to expect."

However, teams should not limit the items to those that emulate the state test. Therefore, short answer, constructed response, and alternative response items can and should be included as well as timed essays. There are a number of ways for determining students' understanding, and the key to actually using assessments formatively is to ensure that the group can determine the next steps of instruction based on the assessments.

The fifth-grade team at Harriet Tubman Elementary decided to redouble their efforts on the strand of English language arts concerning writing strategies. This PLC+ team has already unpacked the standards, developed learning intentions, created success criteria, and mapped out their learning progressions. Thus they easily recognize that, of the five strands of language arts, the writing strategies strand is the one on which the fifth-grade students from the previous year did the worst. During their initial collaborative team meetings, the teachers talked about this particular strand of standards, including what students needed to know and how those standards might be assessed. They also recalled the lack of success students experienced the previous year. Their common challenge centered on the students' development of strong writing strategies articulated in their standards.

As one of the fifth-grade teachers, Ms. Phillips, said, "I need to see the released items. I have no idea how they're going to determine whether students can write a formal introduction, provide supporting evidence, and then develop a conclusion. This isn't fourth grade, when students do an actual writing test. How does anyone know whether students are able to do this in fifth grade?"

As part of the conversation, the teachers shared ideas and materials that they had used in the past to focus on writing strategies. One of the newest teachers at the school, Ms. Javier, commented, "I'm not even sure what writing strategies are. I can help my students write better, but what are the writing strategies they [the authors of the tests] want to see?" A more senior member of the faculty explained the definition for writing strategies used in the state and shared instructional materials he had used. "I'll bring some of my own students' writing samples to our next meeting, and I'll show you some examples of what they are doing."

As a group, the teachers agreed on their pacing guide for the first two months of school and focused their attention on writing strategies and how they would develop this strand with their students. As Ms. James commented at the end of the collaborative team meeting, "Yeah, we have to get better with writing strategies, but let's not forget how good we've become with literary analysis and reading comprehension—we will need to pay attention to that as well."

During their subsequent collaborative team meetings, this group of teachers designed a common assessment and met to discuss the results (see Figure 5.1). Taking heed of Ms. James's comment, the common assessment included items other than writing strategies, as the teachers knew that they were responsible for all of the strands of the language arts. However, a disproportionate number of questions was focused on writing strategies, so that teachers would be able to collect data on their common challenge: Fifth-grade students were not performing as well as they could on the writing strategies section of the assessment.

During their item analysis conversation, they focused on questions 9 through 12 (see Figure 5.2). While discussing question 9, Ms. James

FIGURE 5.1   Sample Common Assessment Items

ORGANIZATION AND FOCUS

Directions: Read the paragraph in the box. Then read each question and the answers carefully. Choose the best answer and mark it. Use what you learn from reading the paragraph to answer questions 9 and 10.

Fire Fighters and Your Safety

Although you may have a smoke detector in your home, fire fighters can help make sure your house is a safe place to live. Fire fighters can make sure your home has escape routes in case a fire occurs. Fire fighters can check for gas leaks in the kitchen. Fire fighters can also install rope ladders in case you need to climb out of a high window.

9. What is the purpose of this paragraph?

    A. To tell us many of the things fire fighters can do for you and your safety

    B. To explain how fire fighters look for escapes in your house

    C. To tell us about the training fire fighters receive

    D. To tell how fire fighters check for gas leaks

10. Which is the best topic sentence for this paragraph?

    A. Fire fighters can install rope ladders in case you need to climb out of a high window.

    B. Fire fighters can make sure your home has escape routes in case a fire occurs.

    C. Fire fighters can help make sure your house is a safe place to live, even if you have a smoke detector in your home.

    D. Fire fighters can check for gas leaks in the kitchen.

RESEARCH AND TECHNOLOGY

Directions: Read each question carefully. Find the correct answer and mark it.

11. The title page of a book gives all but one of the following. Which one does it not give?

    A. The name(s) of the author(s)

    B. Where the publisher's offices are

    C. The name of the publisher

    D. The copyright date

12. Which one is not true for the index of a book?

    A. It may list many pages for the same word or entry.

    B. It is found at the beginning of the book.

    C. It lists entries (words, etc.) in alphabetical order.

    D. It gives page, section, or chapter numbers for entries.

STOP

End of Assessment

FIGURE 5.2   Common Assessment Results

Percentage of students who selected each answer (shaded cell indicates correct response)

Question	Standard	Total Students	A	B	C	D	Blank
9	Strategies 1.0	214	79.91%	10.75%	5.14%	3.74%	0.47%
10	Strategies 1.2a	214	9.81%	21.50%	62.62%	4.67%	1.40%
11	Strategies 1.3	214	21.96%	42.52%	10.75%	22.43%	2.34%
12	Strategies 1.3	214	22.90%	31.31%	32.24%	12.15%	1.40%

TEAM TIME DISCUSSION

Common Challenge

What assessment format(s) will we use?

Items for preunit/postunit assessments

Date of administration of preunit common assessment

Date of team discussion of preunit assessment results (use data analysis protocol in Module 8)

Date of postunit administration of common assessment

Date of team discussion of postunit assessment results (use data visualization tool in Module 16)

COLLABORATIVE WORK WITH YOUR TEAM

Module 17:
Team Time Discussion

page 119 in
The PLC+ Playbook

noted that the fifth graders did relatively well on this item. They seemed to understand purpose of the paragraph. They noted that about 11 percent of the students (about 24 students) chose answer B. Ms. Javier noted that this group of students identified a detail, but not the main idea. Mr. Green indicated that he thought that the classroom teachers could address this in their shared reading lessons. As he said, "Most of our students got this. We need to keep at it. When we're doing our shared readings, we need to pause every so often and talk about the main idea and compare that with the interesting details that the author provides."

Question 10, identifying the topic sentence, was more difficult for this group of fifth graders. While the majority of students answered correctly, significant numbers of students did not. Ms. Phillips suggested that the group that chose answer B, "the almost right answer," meet as part of the reading intervention program. Ms. Phillips offered to focus her push-in intervention groups on reading for information and identifying the topic of a piece of text. Mr. Green agreed, saying, "We didn't hit this one as well. There are a bunch of kids who need help on this. This group needs intervention if they're going to catch on to this." The conversation continued with the team offering Ms. Phillips support for this intervention, including instructional materials and strategies she might find helpful as she attempted to focus on this content standard with students who did not understand this information.

Eventually, the group began talking about questions 11 and 12. Finally Ms. Nguyen voiced what the group seemed to be thinking: "What happened? They totally missed this. I can't believe it. It's like we didn't even teach this stuff. Less than a third of our students can answer these questions right. I'm so frustrated right now."

Ms. James suggested that they "take apart the questions and figure out what they're missing."

"They just picked a correct answer on number 12—they missed the *not,*" Ms. Phillips noted.

Ms. Nguyen sighed and said, "I'm feeling better. I thought that my students really understood the parts of a book. We've been through this. They know so many of the text features and how to use those features when they are reading for information. I just couldn't imagine what was going on."

DETERMINING IMPACT OF INSTRUCTION

We believe that PLC+ team discussions are powerful and have resulted in improved instruction as well as better outcomes for students (e.g., Lai, Wilson, McNaughton, & Hsiao, 2014). In collaborative teams, we identify learning intentions and discuss ideas for instruction, reviewing the literature to see which evidence-based practices might be considered. We meet to review student work and figure out whether our efforts have been fruitful. But this question, "What did we learn today?" requires that we figure out whether students have learned what they were supposed to learn and whether or not our teaching practices facilitated or hindered learning. Without a focus on student learning, the PLC+ discussions might be interesting academic experiences, but not change students' learning. One key to the success of professional learning communities is a focus on impact.

Hattie (2009) maintains that teachers must be able to determine their impact on student learning, and we agree. As we have noted, he uses a statistical tool called effect size to determine the impact that a given influence has on students' learning. Teachers can use the same tool to determine their impact. To calculate an effect size, you subtract the pretest score from the posttest score and then divide by the average of the two standard deviations. This can be quickly done in an Excel spreadsheet. Of course, there are other ways to determine impact, but this was appealing to us; it is consistent and easy to use.

Hattie's effect size list is based on aggregate reviews of other studies to determine the effect that a given process or procedure has on student learning. As an example, statistically combining the effect of grade-level retention as measured through 207 studies involving a total of 13,938 participants reveals a negative effect size of –0.32. An effect size is the magnitude of the influence. In other words, for a given action, how large a response should be expected? Hattie noted that 95 percent of teachers' actions are "effective" when the baseline for growth is zero! *All you need is a pulse!* That means that just about everything we do as teachers has an impact only if measured against a starting point of zero or no growth—no learning—during the year. But if we expect a full year of growth for a year in school, things are very different, and the list of impactful practices is sharply reduced. So when we get a negative effect, such as for retention, then we should be concerned every time we consider holding a student back a year.

Hattie showed that an effect size of 0.40 equated to a year of learning for a year of school. Now that is based on rigorous research design and not typical classroom assessment tools, but the use of effect size calculations can help teachers understand their impact on students' learning, and that understanding, in turn, can guide improvements in instruction.

Here's an example of the use of effect sizes to determine impact.

In a history department, a professional learning community of teachers administered an initial assessment about World War II. They included factual information as well as common misconceptions. For example, some questions were about country membership in the Allied forces versus the Axis powers, and others focused on geography. Still other questions focused on common misconceptions, such as the United States becoming involved in World War II in order to liberate concentration camps. The average for the pretest was only 5 out of 25 correct, and the average for the posttest was 19 out of 25 correct (on different versions of the assessment). Using the effect size tool, the teachers determined their impact, which was 0.77 standard deviations of growth. In addition to finding the average effect size for the class, the teachers looked at the average effect size across race, socioeconomic status, and language minorities. They wanted to ensure that all learners were making learning gains with this content. The teachers concluded that their instruction was generally effective and discussed a number of things that they believed contributed to their success.

As Nathan Knoffler said, "I'm new to U.S. history. I've been teaching world [history] for a long time. The pretest really helped me figure out the misconceptions so that I could work to address those."

Later in the conversation, Maria Sales said, "It was really helpful for me when you all shared the learning intentions. I think my pace was way better this year, because I understood the flow of the unit from our conversations about the expectations for each day." The conversation about their positive impact on student learning was both reinforcing for teachers and growth producing, as individuals considered their instructional repertories.

> As we have emphasized, equity of access and opportunity to learn should be at the forefront of the strategies or approaches selected to move learning forward.

These teachers also replaced the group scores with individual student scores and then calculated the effect sizes for each student using the same statistical analysis. In this way, they were able to note which individual students did not make sufficient progress. This then allowed them to laser in on specific students or groups of students (e.g., students of different socioeconomic status, or gender, race, or language groups) and discuss ways to respond to students who missed the learning intention.

As one teacher noted, "It's really only a few students who didn't make it, which is great and better than before. Given that many students mastered the standards, I think we should organize some peer tutoring. We have done that in the past, and it really worked. Students told us it was fun, and it's not a waste of time for students who already got it." Ms. Sales added, "I also think we might need to review the vocabulary of this lesson. I'm thinking that these words got in the way for some students and that it wouldn't hurt to do a quick review." As we discussed in the previous chapter, the PLC+ collaborative team devoted time to dialoguing about the validity of the selection of specific strategies. Is this the right strategy at the right time? And, as we have emphasized, equity of access and opportunity to learn should be at the forefront of the strategies or approaches selected to move learning forward. The team set out to plan this review and agreed to readminister a postassessment for the students who did not reach mastery on the previous version. As a quick note, this postassessment would assess the same knowledge, skills, and understanding as the first postassessment, but would not simply be a retake of the identical assessment. The teachers want to ensure that learning has occurred and that learners are not simply experiencing a bump in performance due to testing practice.

Determining impact is not at all limited to multiple-choice or constructed response assessments. For example, group of English language arts teachers designed a unit of study on presentation skills. They collaborated on a series of lessons that included focusing on prosody (e.g., intonation, pauses, emphasis) and preparing and practicing speeches. At one of their collaborative team meetings, they compared assessment results. Each teacher had submitted initial assessment scores and averages on the agreed-upon presentation skills rubric, and standard deviations had been calculated. Six weeks later, they collected benchmark data to make decisions about their impact. During their discussion, they noted that their effect size was only 0.30. As one of the teachers commented, "They don't seem to be getting much better at this." This led to a key important discussion about why learners may have missed the mark and what actions could be taken to support those learners.

In their discussion, the teachers reviewed previous efforts and identified several actions that they could take to potentially impact students' learning. The list of actions they agreed to included these:

- Analysis of videos of effective and ineffective public speakers

- Lessons about how formal speeches sound like reading, not like friendly conversations

- Written drafts of speeches that included introduction, body, and conclusion

- Anonymous peer review of written drafts using a computerized program

They spent time sharing ideas with one other. As Melissa Mazur said, "I really learned a lot about helping students present information and ideas. I hadn't thought about modeling a formal speech and then fishbowling a friendly conversation."

Phillip Wade added, "Our plans are much more solid now, and I'm feeling much more confident. In fact, I asked Melissa to spend time

> Determining impact is not at all limited to multiple-choice or constructed response assessments.

in my classroom on her prep so that she could let me know if my lesson on analyzing videos was effective and if she can use it."

When these teachers met again six weeks later to discuss impact, the results were impressive. The average effect size had increased to 0.85, and all but three students had effect sizes that exceeded 0.40. They identified some support they needed from a resource teacher so that that the three students could be successful. They also focused on the changes they made and discussed what they thought were the most effective components. This collective teacher efficacy, based on analyzing the impact that they had on students' learning, resulted in better teaching as well as better learning. Of course, these conversations rested on having good enough assessment tools. We say *good enough* because the tools do not have to meet the psychometric demands that commercial publishers' tools do. They need to measure what they say they measure, and they need to be based on the content being taught. A way to think about it is, "Do they meet the jury standard?" Would twelve peers agree they are assessing what they are intended to assess?

(For more on calculating effect sizes, see "Visualizing Data" on page 122 in Module 18 in *The PLC+ Playbook*.)

COLLABORATIVE WORK WITH YOUR TEAM

Module 18:
Team Time Discussion
page 123 in
The PLC+ Playbook

PROGRESS VERSUS ACHIEVEMENT

Sometimes, team members need to talk about the progress students are making rather than the absolute level of success attained. Of course, our eyes remain focused on learning achievement, but discussions about progress can be useful in helping teams make decisions about what course of action to take. Imagine a student who generally achieves well but is not making progress in a specific unit of study. In most schools, that situation is ignored. But we are missing an opportunity to extend the learning of every student when we fail to monitor both progress and success. One of the ways to visualize the relationship between progress and success is to construct a four-quadrant grid as noted in Figure 5.3.

The amount of progress students make scales left to right, whereas the overall level of achievement scales top to bottom. Of course, this requires that you have some initial assessment data to determine the amount of progress students have made. A student in the upper right-hand box has made a lot of progress and is achieving well. That's cause for celebration; the instructional experiences are working, and the student is learning at high levels. The upper left-hand box suggests students who have achieved well (perhaps because they already knew the content) and are not making further progress. These are students that are often ignored, as the assumption is that they will score well enough on summative assessments. These are students who are neglected by school systems desperately trying to

FIGURE 5.3   Progress/Achievement Grid

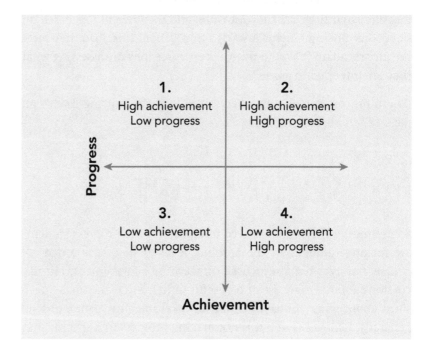

meet the needs of their most struggling learners. But it's unfair to the students in this quadrant. They deserve to make as much progress in their learning as anyone else. Chapter 6 provides more information about supporting, and challenging, students who are achieving well but not making much progress.

The lower two quadrants also represent important discussion points. The lower right-hand quadrant includes students who are not yet achieving but who are making progress. These students are less of a concern, as they are growing in their understanding. They may need some acceleration experiences, but the experiences planned for their learning are generally working. The students in the bottom left quadrant need triage. They are not progressing or achieving. They are at high risk of failing to learn the essential concepts and skills required by the standards. As will be further discussed in Chapter 6, these students might be candidates for supplemental and intensive interventions. But until teachers reflect on their current practice, they can't determine whether students need supplemental and intensive interventions.

The kindergarten teachers at Harriet Beecher Stowe Elementary School used the progress/achievement grid to discuss students' needs. They used the Yopp-Singer Test of Phonemic Segmentation (Yopp, 1995) at the beginning of the school year to identify the skills of every student. Nine weeks into the school year, they administered the assessment again and created a grid with all of the students placed in one of the quadrants. Each teacher was provided a grid with the students in his or her class as well as an aggregate grid with all of the kindergarteners identified.

Matthew Rothstein activated the conversation, starting by asking the teachers to discuss with a partner what they noticed about the grade-level data. The teachers talked with each other, noting that there were a significant number of students in the upper right-hand quadrant. As Marsha Van Landingham said, "I am so happy right now. Our efforts are really paying off. The data did not look like this last year at this time. I hope that they continue to develop, because then we'll be pretty sure that these new instructional materials are working."

The teachers also noted the students who had already reached mastery and could not make any further progress. In assessment circles, this is known as a ceiling effect. The students can't score any higher on the assessment after they get all of the answers correct. Thus, their teachers need to provide other learning opportunities so that time is not wasted for those students who have already demonstrated mastery. But there is a risk in assuming that all students in the upper left quadrant have hit the ceiling. Some students may have achieved well at the time but not made appropriate progress. After all, our expectations should increase as the year progresses.

The teachers placed in the achieving group students who got 8 items correct during the first week of school, but they increased their expectation to 14 items correct nine weeks into the year. Eleanor Larson noted that Ezekiel scored 14 during the first week of school and 14 at the nine-week check-up. He was still in the achieving group, but he had not made progress. She asked the team to talk about him further to determine what might be getting in the way of his learning. His teacher, Grace Flores, responded, "I'm really worried about him. He never comes to school. I've talked with the counselor several times. I think it's time for a home visit so that we can show his mom that he's not making progress. We have to get him to school."

COLLABORATIVE WORK WITH YOUR TEAM

Module 18:
Team Time Discussion
page 124 in
The PLC+ Playbook

The conversation continued, with teachers on the team noting students who were making progress but not yet achieving at the expected level. They noted that most of the students in the lower right quadrant started with 0 items correct, and now they were getting 7 to 10 correct. As Ms. Flores noted, "They started really behind, but they're catching on. I think we should continue to monitor their progress, but I'm not that worried. Once it starts to click, in English, I think that they'll accelerate. I'm more worried about the students who are not achieving and not progressing. I think we need to intervene immediately, before it's too late." The team agreed and shifted to the last question ("Who benefited and who did not benefit?"), so that they could design appropriate interventions for the students who really struggled. However, as you will notice in the next chapter, they proceeded with caution. If we view progress only as students making incremental increases from where they started, a student who is several grades below grade level, who needs learning to be accelerated, might get left behind. Thus, the rate of progress is also an issue that should be addressed. Calculating effect size through examination of pre and post assessment data reduces the possibility that the team will settle for limited progress.

Issues of equity and high expectations inform all the decisions made in a professional learning community. In the chapter that follows, we will turn our attention to analyzing who has benefited from our efforts and who has not. Our collective efforts ultimately center on ensuring that all students are making progress and achieving desired outcomes.

CONCLUSION

When considering the reply to the question "What did we learn today?" PLC+ teams collectively focus and reflect on their implementation of evidence-based instructional practices. This focus guides them closer to addressing the common challenges they face as a team, provides clarity in how they will accomplish their goals, and confirms for them whether they are making an impact. And this is an iterative, cyclical process.

In PLC+ teams, the process of responding to this question, and the pathway to a response, invites teachers into conversations about students' learning as well. We come together and discuss the expectations we have for students and whether those expectations are at least held in common across the grade or department.

When asking, "What did we learn today?" and before taking direct action in the PLC+, we engage in protocols that support reflection on our professional practices that include both teaching and learning. We learned in this chapter that reflection requires consciously examining and thinking about our experiences, actions, feelings, and responses, and then interpreting or analyzing them in order to learn from them (Atkins & Murphy, 1994; Boud et al., 1994). True reflection connects our new learning with actions moving forward. We need to be able to process and articulate our new learning. We also need to learn how to determine our impact, and how to write effective pre and post assessments. Last, we need to consider student progress versus student achievement and make decisions together regarding how to act upon various student needs, so that *all* learners' needs are addressed.

The table that follows identifies the key ideas from this chapter organized around the four crosscutting values. In addition, there are reflection questions your team can use to ensure that your efforts are resulting in equity and high expectations for all students, while also building individual and collective efficacy. Of course, activators are important for accomplishing all of these goals.

EQUITY	This is fundamentally about access and opportunities to learn. As mentioned in this chapter, it is important for PLC+ team members to look at both student progress and growth, and it is equally important to also share that information with the student. This could support establishing learning goals as students move forward. One of the ways students can propel their progress and achievement is through utilizing effective learning strategies that challenge their thinking, make personal connections, and value their cultural backgrounds. The key is to make sure students are not only aware of those strategies but know when and where to use them. • How does your PLC+ currently look at both progress and achievement in student learning? • In what ways does your PLC+ ensure that not only are students aware of learning strategies, but they know when and where to use them in their learning? • How could expert noticing drive equity in student learning? • How does your PLC+ ensure that all students have access to meaningful and effective instruction?
HIGH EXPECTATIONS	The establishment of high expectations for student learning is critical, and as mentioned previously, this will oftentimes begin with looking at the skills, concepts, and rigor level within a standard. Yet designing learning tasks that connect to those expectations as well as scoring student work against those expectations are additional layers that need to have a place within your PLC+. Reflection can also invite students into the process of understanding their current progress against the expectations that have been established. When assessment results come back to PLC+ teams, they must ensure expectations maintain high levels as being the constant. How they will move all students to these levels can be the variable. • How can collaborative analysis of student work within your PLC+ support equity in expectations? • What strategies does your PLC+ currently use to support reflection? • What is the link between assessment design within your PLC+ and student expectations?

INDIVIDUAL AND COLLECTIVE EFFICACY	Learning together as a collective whole is one way to drive efficacy, both at the individual and collective level. It is critical to ensure that the learning your PLC+ is engaging in is connected to the adult learning needs identified to better support the student learning needs identified. This can oftentimes be identified through PLC+ reflection. Learning as a collective capitalizes on the expertise of each member of the PLC+. • In what ways do you currently engage in new learning with your PLC+? • How could development of expert noticing within your PLC+ support development of individual and collective efficacy? • Does your team collectively own the responsibility for the results you are currently seeing as well as for what you expect to see on growth for all of your students moving forward?
ACTIVATION	Effectively analyzing student performance data within a PLC+ can oftentimes be a challenge. There will always be one teacher whose data are the "highest" and one whose are "lowest." The critical factor is to look at the data in terms of *impact*. PLC+ teams need to constantly engage in discourse around the learning tasks they engineered, the strategies they used to support students in engaging in those tasks, and, as a result, how well students performed against the established learning intentions. • What do you think are key attributes of an activator who can facilitate a PLC+ discussion where teachers feel okay to be vulnerable? • What is the link between effective facilitation and genuine reflection? • How can the activator create an environment of trust so that people can talk honestly about the data?

EQUITY AND EXPECTATIONS VALUES CHECKLIST

QUESTION	MY THOUGHTS	OUR COLLECTIVE THOUGHTS
Did we take time to reflect on students' learning?		
Did we take time to reflect on our own learning?		
What evidence do we have about students' learning?		
Have we developed and administered common assessments that will allow us to determine mastery and needs for additional learning?		
What did we learn about our impact on students?		
What did the progress versus achievement exercise teach us?		
What do we need to modify in our plan that will allow us to address the common challenge?		

ACTIVATE LEARNING FOR MYSELF AND OTHERS CHECKLIST

Student learning needs drive adult learning needs. Once teams understand where students are now in their learning journey, teams need to take a step back to reflect on their personal learning. Are there any adult learning needs that must be met to best be able to support student learning? As already discussed, the + in the PLC+ is you, and so it is important to recognize learning for teachers is a constant. Given that you want to move student learning forward, what learning do you (or your team) need to accomplish to ensure that all students are successful?

WHAT DID WE NOTICE AS OUR STUDENTS ENGAGED IN THIS LEARNING UNIT?	WHAT ARE MY LEARNING NEEDS SO I CAN MEET MY STUDENTS' LEARNING NEEDS? What strategies might I need to learn more about?	WHAT LEARNING WILL I ENGAGE IN TO MEET MY LEARNING NEEDS? What will I do on my own? What can I do with colleagues?

COLLABORATIVE WORK WITH YOUR TEAM

Module 19:
Equity and Expectations Values Checklist
page 128 in
The PLC+ Playbook

Module 19:
Activate Learning for Myself and Others Checklist
page 129 in
The PLC+ Playbook

Module 19:
Collective Efficacy Checklist
page 130 in
The PLC+ Playbook

COLLECTIVE EFFICACY CHECKLIST

Teams that are empowered to make decisions, act, communicate clearly, and hold themselves accountable for their efforts manifest high degrees of collective teacher efficacy (CTE). Use the checklist below to gauge and monitor the actions that will follow your work about the fourth question, "What did we learn today?"

QUESTION	MY THOUGHTS	OUR COLLECTIVE THOUGHTS
How confident are we in the assessments we used to determine students' progress?		
Do we believe that our team and our school are moving in a positive direction to improve student learning?		
How has our team's learning transformed to teacher practice?		
What experiences do we need to have to extend our sense of collective efficacy?		

QUESTION 5:
Who BENEFITED and Who DID NOT BENEFIT?

PLC+ Framework Guiding Questions

1. **Where are we going?**
2. **Where are we now?**
3. **How do we move learning forward?**
4. **What did we learn today?**
5. **Who benefited and who did not benefit?**

THE STORY BEHIND THE QUESTION

This final question in the PLC+ framework takes a critical look at who did and did not make the expected learning gains as a result of our instruction. And, to truly answer the question of benefit, we have to refocus on the learning intentions, success criteria, and learning progressions that provide the definition of benefit. What makes this question so vital to the PLC+ framework is also what makes this question challenging and uncomfortable. PLC+ teams must confront the evidence that points to learners that did not benefit from their instruction and the potential commonalities among these learners. As you will see later in this chapter, one of the aspects of this question asks if learning experiences provided to those underperforming learners are of the same quality as those provided to high-performing learners.

Effective activation through facilitation of such challenging conversations is paramount. As you will see in this chapter, PLC+ team

Video 7
Introduction to Chapter 6

resources.corwin.com/
plcplus

members must look at trends and patterns in both growth and achievement. Are there common characteristics of learners not experiencing growth or achievement? This could support establishing supplemental and intensive interventions to provide **equity** of access and opportunity for all learners. Engaging in these conversations can surface teachers' limiting assumptions about the capabilities of students as well as barriers to learning (e.g., irrelevant learning experiences). Doing so can also help eliminate barriers to learning, especially when dedicated teachers identify these issues and then work to address them.

> If the team does not have immediate expertise to address a common challenge, there must be professional learning that builds that expertise.

Furthermore, are **expectations** of and for learning held constant for all? Reflecting on who did and who did not benefit will maintain our expectations for both growth and achievement, but at the same time will help reveal who is and who is not making those gains. And *why* they are not. Recognizing those learners who did not benefit from instruction should prompt our PLC+ to engage in professional learning about supporting all learners. If the team does not have immediate expertise to address a common challenge, there must be professional learning that builds that expertise—and thus enhances the **individual and collective efficacy** of the PLC+.

A PLC+ TEAM IN ACTION

Loretta Wright and her teachers at Williams Elementary School are committed to successfully implementing PLC+s. Together with her assistant principal, Ms. Wright has devoted a lot of time to building the individual and collective efficacy of her teachers, as well as the activation skills of the teachers who lead those teams. "We have worked very hard to build the activation skills of our teachers so that they have the efficacy to activate their PLC+ collaborative team meetings." In the end, this capacity building has paid off, as some of her grade-level teams must tackle one of the more emotionally difficult questions in the PLC+ framework: Who benefited from the teaching and who did not benefit? Hopefully, teachers have been monitoring students' progress throughout the unit of study and have made adjustments along the way. Still, being confronted with trend data that indicate that some students did not learn is hard.

One of the teachers, Ronda Morris, shares that "now that I know the what, how, and why of our collaborative team meetings and we have developed trust, and I see these conversations make a difference for my students, I'm more comfortable to share who has not benefited from my instruction. After all, if something isn't working, I have to address that something. This is easier when my entire team can chip in with help and support." This particular component of the PLC+ model takes the previous question, "What did we learn today?" and narrows in on the trends and patterns in student learning. And, when necessary, this focus should narrow in on specific learners who have not fully benefited from instruction, and who need more targeted teaching or instructional intervention.

Specifically, Rachel Lancaster and her second-grade team are engaging in a critical analysis of reading growth across the previous two weeks. The second-grade team has identified reading as their problem of practice. Although broad, this common challenge is derived from the negative trend in reading growth and performance across grade levels that they have experienced for the last two years. In addition to the pre and post assessment data, teachers are looking closely at students' running records. Ms. Lancaster shares with her colleagues the data grid that looks at both growth and achievement (Figure 6.1).

FIGURE 6.1 Growth and Achievement Reading Data

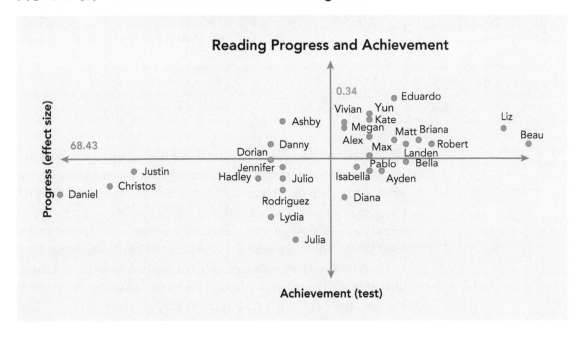

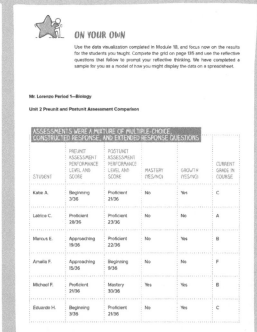

Module 20:
On Your Own
page 132 in
The PLC+ Playbook

Module 20:
On Your Own
page 136 in
The PLC+ Playbook

We introduced this grid in Chapter 5, but we will use it here to move us deeper into examining the results, as they pertain to equity, of what we do each day in our classrooms. For Ms. Lancaster, this grid was generated from the pre and post assessment scores for the most recent unit in reading. "I've entered the postassessment data for my kiddos. How they appear on the grid is both interesting and, to be honest, a bit disheartening. I am really interested in talking through the bottom left quadrant. This group of learners has me very worried, and I am looking for ways to support these learners." This deliberate focus on learning is supported by the common challenge identified by the teachers and the data to provide insight into the challenge—cautiously navigating biases.

Students are placed in one of the four quadrants based on their achievement score as well as their growth or progress over the past unit. Achievement scores are a reality of today's schools and classrooms. However, Ms. Lancaster, and all of the teachers and administrators at Williams Elementary School, focus on growth. The principal, Ms. Wright, points out that "if we focus our attention on maximizing learning gains and growth, in the end, the achievement scores will take care of themselves." Let's take a moment and walk through each of the quadrants shown on Ms. Lancaster's grid so that we, alongside her PLC+ team, can make meaning of the data and determine who benefited and who did not benefit.

Starting in the upper right quadrant, these are learners that exceeded the achievement benchmark and demonstrated above average growth in reading (Figure 6.2).

FIGURE 6.2   Students in the High-Growth and High-Achievement Quadrant

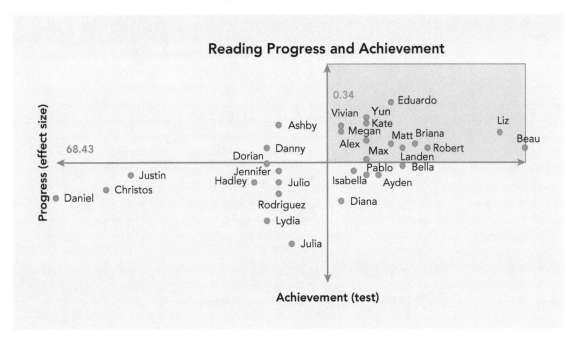

For example, not only did Eduardo, Yun, Kate, Liz, and Beau exceed the achievement benchmark, represented by the horizontal line, but they also demonstrated high levels of progress, beyond average growth, represented by the vertical line. The combination of high growth and high achievement is the desire of every stakeholder in education.

Let's move to the bottom left quadrant (Figure 6.3). "The tasks that I designed to improve their expository writing did not seem to have any effect on these learners," Ms. Lancaster says. "For many learners, their writing now is no better than it was at the start of this unit. I have to find a way to connect with them. What I've been doing isn't working for these children. I have made several adjustments over the past several weeks based on the data, but I think I need help."

Daniel, Julia, Lydia, and others showed no growth and minimal achievement. In fact, many of the learners in this quadrant showed negative growth. This requires Ms. Lancaster and her team to take immediate action to identify why these learners did not post either high achievement scores or growth in this content. One immediate

FIGURE 6.3   Students in the Low-Growth and Low-Achievement Quadrant

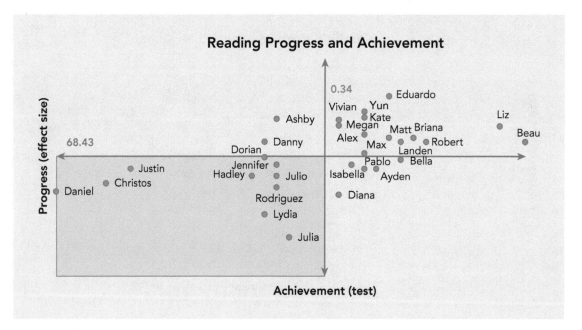

question might be what Ms. Lancaster knows about Daniel, Julia, Lydia, and the other learners in this quadrant as people, not just as learners. This is the essence of this particular component of the PLC+ framework. When looking at who benefited and who did not benefit, we have to zero in on trends and patterns in student learning outcomes—in terms of both achievement and growth. What about this particular instructional lesson or lessons made them so ineffective in growth and achievement for Daniel, Julia, or Lydia?

Along those same lines, how is the learning different for learners that experienced high achievement, but no growth? Ashby and Danny, highlighted in Figure 6.4, exceeded the achievement benchmark but actually regressed in their growth.

Finally, there is a group of learners who are benefitting from instruction. They have made considerable progress. But, given their overall achievement, they appear not to be successful. Find Diana, Bella, or Isabella on the grid. These students, along with Pablo and Ayden, showed high growth but did not cross the benchmark (Figure 6.5). In most districts, schools, and classrooms, these learners would fall into the "did not

FIGURE 6.4   Students in the Low-Growth and High-Achievement Quadrant

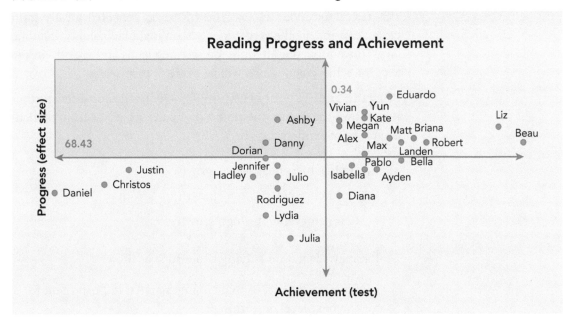

FIGURE 6.5   Students in the High-Growth and Low-Achievement Quadrant

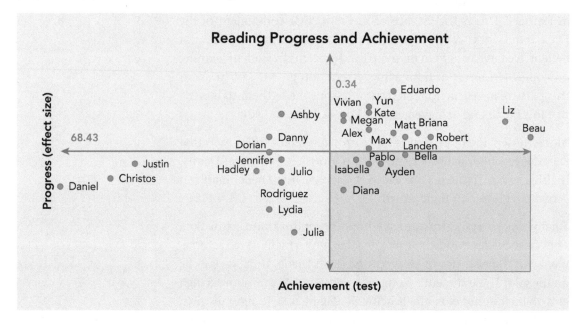

Reading Progress and Achievement

pass" category and are assumed to be struggling students. However, a more deliberate, intentional, and purposeful analysis of who benefited and who did not reveals that these learners *demonstrated high growth.* This fact alone indicates that these learners benefited greatly from instruction and are the very students Ms. Wright talks about when she says, "If we focus our attention on learning gains and growth, in the end, the achievement scores will take care of themselves."

Using this grid, we want to take this PLC+ conversation a step further and address the deeper question: What patterns exist within particular groups of learners . . .

- High achievement—low growth
- Low achievement—low growth
- Low achievement—high growth

. . . that may suggest underlying issues such as these:

- Boredom or lack of challenging material to push them to the next level of learning

- Lack of access to materials or tasks that allow students to move into deeper levels of conceptual learning and transfer of learning

- Lack of access to instruction that enables students to master grade-level standards, or limited small group instruction to meet targeted needs

- Institutional barriers (e.g., lack of access to instructional materials) to the learning

- Instruction that fails to address specific learning gaps related to learning progressions students need to reach larger curriculum aims

- Not enough instructional time devoted to allow for guided as well as independent practice to allow students to better grasp subskills needed to progress toward the standards or objectives

Finally, we want to address the deeper question: How do we respond to this analysis of benefit?

To fully address the final question of the PLC+ framework, teams may choose to engage in an equity audit, implement a tiered system of support, engage in additional professional learning, modify instruction, or identify a new common challenge and allocate resources to that.

EQUITY AUDIT

When addressing who benefited and who did not benefit from our instruction, we have to have an honest, candid, and at times uncomfortable conversation about the *who*. Academic data, consensus scoring, task and assignment analysis, and data-informed decisions require us to assess what we learned about the teaching and learning in our classroom. The *who* did and did not benefit addresses the level of equity in both access and opportunity to the learning in our classrooms. This is an audit of the equity within this classroom and grade level. For Ms. Lancaster and her grade-level team, they must move beyond the holistic approach to data analysis (e.g., 65 percent of my learners meet the benchmark, or 18 out of 20 are on grade level) to the trends and patterns within the 65 percent and 35 percent. Let's return to the grid from Ms. Lancaster's classroom (Figure 6.6) and organize the data a bit differently for this discussion.

FIGURE 6.6   Holistic Approach to Growth and Achievement Data

High Achievement— High Growth	High Achievement— Low Growth	Low Achievement— High Growth	Low Achievement— Low Growth
Beau, Liz, Max, Briana, Landon, Robert, Matt, Alex, Megan, Vivian, Kate, Yun, and Eduardo	Danny and Ashby	Bella, Isabella, Ayden, Pablo, and Diana	Daniel, Christos, Justin, Dorian, Jennifer, Hadley, Julio, Rodriguez, Lydia, and Julia

During the PLC+ collaborative team meeting, this team must look at the characteristics of those that did versus those that did not benefit. In many PLC+ collaborative team meetings, this grid points to a new common challenge or problem of practice. In other words, what are we going to do to address the challenge highlighted by the trends and patterns in the data?

Ms. Lancaster takes the lead and asks the first question about these characteristics. "I brainstormed a list of things to consider when looking at the learners in each quadrant for this unit. I would like to talk about each of these with regard to achievement and growth." Ms. Lancaster shares her list, written carefully in the margin of her grid:

> The takeaway message from this audit is not that there is something wrong with learners in each of the above columns. There is no deficit in these learners.

1. Attendance

2. Interest

3. Transience or mobility

4. Gender

5. Socioeconomic status

6. Race

7. Ethnicity

8. Disability status (IEP and 504)

9. English language learners

As Ms. Lancaster and her team move through each quadrant of the grid, they engage in reflective questioning and discussion about how each background or demographic characteristic may have played out in the classroom. In Figure 6.7, we walk through some of the questions and provide examples of what this looked like in Ms. Lancaster's PLC+ and might look like in your next PLC+ discussion. For Figure 6.7, the overarching goal is to see whether the learning experiences provided to those in the lower left quadrant are of the same quality as the experiences provided to those in the upper right quadrant. Are expectations held constant for students in all quadrants?

Before we move forward, there are two areas we want to address in this equity audit. The takeaway message from this audit is not that there is something wrong with learners in each of the columns in Figure 6.6. There is no deficit in these learners. Instead, the deficit lies in our ability, as teachers, to capitalize on the strengths of all learners and provide an inclusive environment where all learners have equitable access to the learning. No exceptions! As uncomfortable as this conversation may be, with the level of vulnerability high, we must have the courage to look at student learning, and thus our teaching, through the lens of equity. For example,

- Are we really offering every single learner equity of access and opportunity for all learning intentions and success criteria?

- Have we maintained high expectations for all students regardless of where learning began?

- Are there institutional barriers that are hindering the growth of some students?

- Are any students pulled out during key times of instruction? If so, who?

EQUITY AUDIT PROTOCOL: REVISIT THE DATA AS A TEAM

Using the individual results you and your team members prepared, discuss the results you have found and the questions you would like to pose to your colleagues. Because there are often patterns in findings, it is wise to begin with a roundtable of results and questions. The appointed activator for this data analysis is charged with keeping the process moving forward. If there is a team member who does not have direct classroom responsibilities, he or she can serve as the activator.

Step 1: Roundtable: Each team member briefly shares the results of his or her analysis with the group. Use the notes you prepared to support your presentation of the data. (3 minutes for each participant)

- Number of students who made progress and demonstrated mastery
- Number of students who made progress but did not demonstrate mastery
- Number of students who did not make progress and demonstrated mastery
- Number of students who did not make progress and did not demonstrate mastery
- One or two patterns you discovered in your analysis
- One question you have for the team

NOTES

_____

_____

_____

_____

_____

_____

_____

_____

_____

_____

_____

_____

---

overview in the roundtable, identify common themes related to results, as well as questions that resonate with the group. (5 minutes)

COMMON THEMES

1.

2.

3.

QUESTIONS RAISED BY THE DATA

1.

2.

3.

Step 3: Dig Deeper to Uncover Patterns of Inequality: Use the questions listed below to reexamine your data in light of possible patterns. While some of the more common patterns are often identified early on (e.g., patterns among the scores of English learners), others may appear later and shed new light on your results (e.g., patterns that are related to attendance). (30 minutes)

CHARACTERISTIC	EQUITY GUIDING QUESTION	EMERGING PATTERNS
Attendance	Do the learners within each quadrant have similar attendance habits? Challenges with truancy or tardiness?	
Interest	How do the learners' explicit or implicit interests in reading correspond to the quadrants?	
Transience and Mobility	Are learners that joined the class late or later in the year experiencing the same achievement and growth as those students that have been members of the class/school the entire year or years?	
Gender	What is the distribution of males and females across the quadrants?	
Socioeconomic Status	Are children in poverty showing differential levels of achievement and or growth?	
Race	What is the distribution of races across the quadrants?	
Ethnicity	How does the ethnic makeup of the grade level show up in each quadrant?	
Disability Status (IEP and 504)	Do students with an identified disability progress and achieve in this classroom and grade level?	
English Language Learners	Are children learning English as a subsequent language showing differential levels of achievement and/or growth?	

Step 4: Examine Issues of Access: Some students fail to make progress, or fail to master content, due to issues of access. These are not always apparent, but they can be pervasive. There is a saying that "the last thing a fish notices is the water it swims in," and so it can be with barriers to access. Take time to interrogate these less obvious access issues that can interfere with and inhibit student growth and learning. (20 minutes)

QUESTION	MY THOUGHTS	OUR COLLECTIVE THOUGHTS
Are we really offering each learner equitable access and opportunity for all learning intentions and success criteria?		
Have we maintained high expectations for all students regardless of where learning began?		
Are there organizational or institutional barriers that are hindering the growth of some?		

Step 5: Use Results, Patterns, and Access to Address the Common Challenge: Your team's further analysis of the results of your efforts, especially through an equity lens, will naturally prompt discussion of responses. We ask that you pause before developing future plans, in order to return to your common challenge. (15 minutes)

Common Challenge

QUESTION	MY THOUGHTS	OUR COLLECTIVE THOUGHTS
Who is currently benefiting from our instruction?		
Who is not benefiting from our instruction?		
What do these results suggest as they relate to our common challenge?		
What questions remain related to our common challenge?		

Step 6: How Do We Strengthen Our Practice? Results are feedback to you about the impact of your teaching (Hattie, 2012). Although this can be a sensitive topic, it is vital to address it in your journey as an effective educator. Imagine what would happen if a doctor never bothered to find out whether his or her patients responded favorably to treatment! Discuss how the results are prompting reflection about your individual practice, and that of the PLC+ team as a whole. (20 minutes)

QUESTION	MY THOUGHTS	OUR COLLECTIVE THOUGHTS
What are the implications for our individual practice?		
In what ways might these results inform future inquiry by our team?		
What have we learned that can strengthen our PLC+ moving forward?		

Step 7: What Actions Are We Compelled to Take on Behalf of Students? In light of your investigation of the data, what action steps will your PLC+ team take to improve future student learning? *Any one of these goals holds the potential of being your next common challenge.* (20 minutes)

GOALS	PROPOSED ACTION	INTERNAL SUPPORTS WE WILL NEED	EXTERNAL SUPPORTS WE WILL NEED	DATE TO REVISIT (MONITOR PROGRESS)
To improve equitable access to content				
To improve teacher clarity				
To improve teacher credibility				
To strengthen expectations				
To remove organizational or institutional barriers				

COLLABORATIVE WORK WITH YOUR TEAM

Module 20:
Equity Audit Protocol:
Revisit the Data as a Team
pages 137–143 in *The PLC+ Playbook*

FIGURE 6.7 Potential Background and Demographic Characteristics in the Classroom

Characteristic	Equity Guiding Questions	Possible Scenarios or Examples From Ms. Lancaster's PLC+
Attendance	Do the learners within each quadrant have similar attendance habits? Challenges with truancy or tardiness?	Should Ms. Lancaster and her team find that those learners with high achievement and no growth have a significantly higher number of absences, they should find out why. It may be that these learners do not find value added by attending the school. The team might then address ways to make sure time in class contributes to the achievement and growth of learners. Furthermore, is the team gathering more information about why certain students are not coming to school?
Interest	How do the learners' explicit or implicit interests in reading correspond to the quadrants?	This PLC+ might discuss the possibility that only those learners interested in the selected reading materials demonstrate high growth—regardless of the achievement. They might look for opportunities to increase interest in reading. In addition, how can the team build positive and productive relationships with their students?
Transience and mobility	Are learners that joined the class late or later in the year experiencing the same achievement and growth as those students that have been members of the class/school the entire year or years?	One of Ms. Lancaster's colleagues points out that learners who join the class after the first few weeks of school are in the low-growth quadrants. The team might work on ways to assimilate new learners into the classroom culture, develop plans to accelerate learning, and identify prerequisite skills.
Gender	What is the distribution of males or females across the quadrants?	Given that females are overrepresented in the high-achievement categories in the quadrants, the team might focus on ensuring that the content is just as interesting and engaging to males as it is to females. They might also look at prerequisite skills and motivation.
Socioeconomic status	Are children in poverty showing differential levels of achievement and/or growth?	The achievement gap at Williams Elementary School is greatest along socioeconomic lines. The team should explore why this is the case and how to support those learners in reading.

Characteristic	Equity Guiding Questions	Possible Scenarios or Examples From Ms. Lancaster's PLC+
Race	What is the distribution of races across the quadrants?	The team notices that black males do not achieve and grow at the same rate as their peers. This racial divide requires the team to openly discuss the reasons behind such an achievement gap.
Ethnicity	How does the ethnic makeup of the grade level show up in each quadrant?	Ms. Lancaster's team notices that their Latinx students post excellent growth. This level of growth is the highest in the school. They engage in close progress monitoring so that they are able to attribute this success to specific decisions they make in their PLC+.
Disability status (IEP and 504)	Do students with an identified disability progress and achieve in this classroom and grade level?	This PLC+ team notices that learners with identified disabilities achieve and grow at high levels in one of their classrooms, but not in all of the second-grade classrooms. This provides a professional learning opportunity led by this particular team member.
English language learners	Are children learning English as a second language showing differential levels of achievement and/or growth?	Williams Elementary School has a growing number of English language learners. In second grade, these learners receive support that supports their achievement and growth, but they are still not evenly distributed over the four quadrants. In fact, Ms. Lancaster notes that these learners are the lowest-performing group. The exception is those learners that were integrated into an English-speaking school earlier in their educational trajectory.

- Is tracking going on within the classroom? If so, why?

- What are our grouping practices? What is our rationale for these practices, and how are we monitoring the impact of them?

- Are needed resources provided? . . . *specifically for students who are most in need of support?*

These are important reflection questions for teachers and teams to struggle with. To be very clear, each of the individual student characteristics in Figure 6.7, in and of itself, does not prevent learning. Instead, the characteristics require us to address and remove barriers to the learning. We do this by removing identified barriers to learning and by implementing approaches like Response to Intervention.

RESPONSE TO INTERVENTION

Response to Intervention, or RTI, is a multitier approach to learning. In some places, it is known as *tiered interventions,* and in other places it is referred to as *multitiered systems of support.* For convenience, we use RTI as a generic phrase to refer to supplemental and intensive supports provided to students who do not respond to the quality core instruction that is provided. Importantly, for some students, intervention may not be the answer. Instead, they need specific barriers to learning to be removed.

RTI provides learners with interventions at increasing levels of intensity (the tiers) based on specific needs. As you might suspect, these needs are identified by progress monitoring, constant checks for understanding, and the collecting of evidence of learning through assessments. There are two big ideas about RTI to keep in mind:

Individual student characteristics do not prevent learning. Instead, the characteristics require us to address and remove barriers to the learning.

1. RTI should not be viewed as a remedy to inequities. Instead, RTI should be viewed as a system of support for learners that are not making the expected gains in their learning.

2. RTI is based on the assumption that classroom teachers know and implement high-quality instruction in their classrooms. Therefore, first, PLC+ teams should gather evidence of implementation of evidence-based practices or high-quality instruction as suggested in the previous questions of the PLC+ framework.

What is paramount in the successful implementation of RTI is the idea that learning outcomes are held constant, but we vary the time and instruction associated with that learning. Let's return to Ms. Lancaster's grid and put this in the context of her first-grade learners (Figure 6.8).

FIGURE 6.8 Students in the High-Growth and Low-Achievement Quadrant

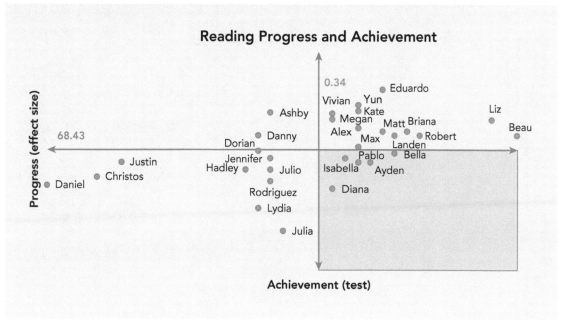

Recall that Diana and four of her peers demonstrated high growth but less than expected achievement. Through the lens of RTI, we do not compromise the ultimate learning, the goal of proficiency or mastery of a learning outcome. This is the belief that all students can and will learn. Instead, the time or rate of learning is adjusted based on the data collected by Ms. Lancaster and her PLC+ team. Given the high growth shown by these five learners, they are clearly benefiting from instruction. The PLC+ members possess the data to provide a multitier system of support for learners like Diana who need adjustments in the time to meet the learning intentions. On the other hand, Daniel, Lydia, and Julia are in a different situation (Figure 6.9), but a situation that can also be adapted through RTI.

These ten learners in the lower left quadrant show both low achievement and little growth. Again, some of them showed negative growth (e.g., Daniel, Christos, and Justin). As with every learner in our schools and classrooms, Ms. Lancaster and her team will not water down or sidestep the learning in this situation. After

FIGURE 6.9   Students in the Low-Growth and Low-Achievement Quadrant

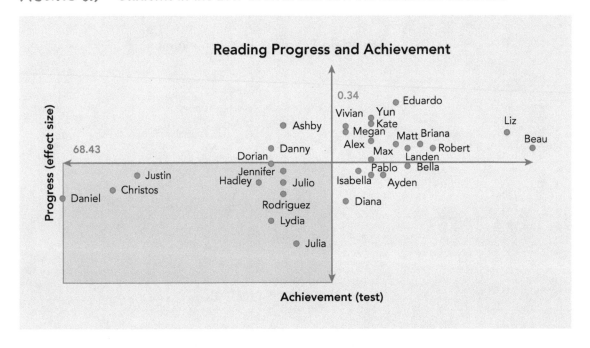

Ms. Lancaster and her PLC+ have ensured that learners were provided with high-quality instruction through evidence-based practices, the data suggest that these learners need interventions to both accelerate the learning and increase the level of performance for each student. Notice the implication of the previous sentence. If these learners need interventions, teachers must provide them. Furthermore, these interventions must not be louder, longer, and more of the same, but a change in how we teach. This also applies to Ashby and Danny, our high-achieving but no-growth learners. Thus, it may be more appropriate to refer to the *I* in RTI as both intervention and instruction.

When correctly implemented, RTI ensures that we notice students who fail to respond to high-quality instruction and that their needs are addressed, while we also keep them included in core instruction. Let's look at several of the factors necessary to implement an effective RTI system of support and how these factors play a pivotal role in the PLC+ framework.

UNIVERSAL SCREENING AND ONGOING ASSESSMENT

In addition to progress monitoring, checks for understanding, and formative assessments, we must have assessments in place to identify where our students are now. This particular component of the PLC+ framework, addressed in a previous chapter, is critical to the understanding of who benefited and who did not benefit. In districts and schools that successfully use a multitiered system of support, all students are initially assessed to determine who might need supplemental or intensive interventions right away. These screening tools should be quick and fairly easy to use, because they are going to be administered to all students. As such, these tools are not expected to be diagnostic and might unintentionally identify students who really do not need an intervention. Keep in mind that a screening tool merely identifies students who are working below grade level; these tools cannot assess what has been tried in the past instructionally and whether it has been successful or not.

A screening tool merely identifies students who are working below grade level; these tools cannot assess what has been tried in the past instructionally and whether it has been successful or not.

In a multitiered system of support, ongoing assessment allows us to evaluate the benefits of specific interventions or the impact of the instructional core curriculum on each individual learner. For example, such ongoing progress monitoring gives Ms. Lancaster access to information about her most recent instructional episodes that will help her make immediate adjustments to instruction, including the rate of expected learning.

Some schools develop course competencies (i.e., learning intentions and success criteria) and assessments that are tightly aligned to the competencies and used formatively; this continuous monitoring allows for intervention for students showing early signs of struggle in a particular course. Students who do not demonstrate competency on one of these assessments are provided with interventions at increasing levels of support, with teachers adjusting the intensity and duration of interventions based on the personalized needs of the student. The school's competencies serve as curriculum-based assessment, meaning that there is "direct observation and recording of a student's performance in the local curriculum as a basis for gathering information to make instructional decisions" (Deno, 1987, p. 41). These tools allow teachers to determine whether students are making progress in the regular curriculum of the course.

Progress monitoring systems commonly used in middle and high schools can challenge an RTI effort. In many schools, students can only receive supplemental and intensive interventions based on their performance in reading or mathematics. In fact, nearly all formal progress monitoring tools focus on reading and mathematics, meaning that other content areas are not reviewed. However, when teachers across the disciplines develop course competencies, progress monitoring occurs in every classroom, and every teacher becomes involved in the RTI process. Successful implementation of RTI requires ongoing assessment and high-quality instruction.

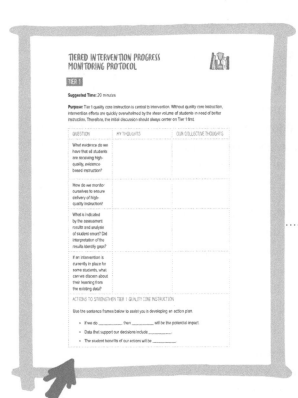

HIGH—QUALITY TIER 1 INSTRUCTION

The RTI system is built on the idea that all teachers implement and all students receive high-quality instruction. At least 85 percent of students should experience success in Tier 1, core instruction. If that is not the case, then school improvement efforts should focus on this level of instruction. To be blunt, bad instruction should not be covered up by having a majority of learners receiving a tiered system of support. From our perspective, the PLC+ framework provides the opportunity for collaborative teams to gather evidence about the implementation of high-quality instruction. At minimum, students in Tier 1 instruction should (Fisher & Frey, 2010):

- Know what they are expected to learn

- Have their teachers model for them

COLLABORATIVE WORK WITH YOUR TEAM

Module 21:
Tiered Intervention Progress Monitoring Protocol
page 146 in
The PLC+ Playbook

- Engage in productive group work

- Have their errors and misconceptions addressed using prompts and cues rather than direct explanations

- Be held individually accountable for their learning

When looking at Ms. Lancaster's data, are 85 percent of her learners benefiting from her instruction? That is, are 85 percent of her learners making progress? During her PLC+ collaborative team meeting, this conversation, as uncomfortable as it may be for everyone, is vital in breaking down the barriers or biases that may be preventing Ms. Lancaster from having a greater impact on student learning.

SUPPLEMENTAL AND INTENSIVE INTERVENTIONS

Once student needs are identified, whether through universal screening or progress monitoring, intervention services must be delivered and monitored. In an RTI^2 model, there are typically two levels of intervention: supplemental and intensive.

Supplemental interventions are those that are delivered in a small group setting, with a group of students who have similar instructional needs. These small groups are not permanent ability groups. Rather, they are teacher led and are temporarily formed to target a specific skill or concept. Supplemental interventions occur at least three times per week for 30 minutes, but many students need more support than that. In essence, supplemental intervention focuses on students' needs and ensures that they have additional direct and guided instruction aligned with those needs. Returning to Ms. Lancaster's PLC+ collaborative team meeting, this would be the starting point for the students in the low achievement–low growth quadrant. After looking at the evidence that she has utilized evidence-based practices, they discussed ways to increase the benefit of their instruction through small group interventions for some of the learners in first grade. For example, the team considered providing small group instruction for Julia, Lydia, Rodriguez, Julio, Hadley, and Jennifer (Figure 6.10).

However, they recognize that Daniel, Christos, and Justin may need more intensive interventions.

Supplemental interventions are those that are delivered in a small group setting, with a group of students who have similar instructional needs. These small groups are not permanent ability groups.

Here is an example of what supplemental instruction might look like in a secondary school. Chad Michelson's high school English class is reading *To Kill a Mockingbird*. For some learners, this is a challenging text, especially when the author seeks to characterize certain witnesses during the trial of Tom Robinson. Mr. Michelson meets three times a week for supplemental interventions with learners who struggle with reading. Today, Mr. Michelson devotes time to building their understanding of author's purpose—how does Harper Lee's characterization of certain witnesses influence the reader's perceptions of their

FIGURE 6.10   **Students in the Low-Growth and Low-Achievement Quadrant**

credibility? He uses this small group time to relate author's purpose and characterization to television commercials and political ads. He then teaches his learners annotation strategies to scaffold their thinking about the specific chapter in *To Kill a Mockingbird*.

Unlike supplemental interventions, *intensive interventions* are delivered individually and are typically reserved for students who are significantly below grade level, often focusing on basic skills and access to the core curriculum. Returning back to Mr. Michelson's classroom, he also meets individually with several students to provide systematic and explicit instruction around author's purpose, context clues, and characterization. Furthermore, while other learners are working independently, Mr. Michelson supports these individuals by having them mirror skills taught during the minilesson or whole group instruction. At times, Max Carson, the special educator, provides this support.

Both supplemental and intensive interventions need to be monitored. At minimum, assessment data should be collected bimonthly (if not weekly) for students receiving supplemental interventions, and weekly (if not daily) for students receiving intensive interventions. Assessment information should be reviewed by an appropriately constructed committee, not only the individuals providing the intervention, so that trends can be identified and discussed, and alternatives can be proposed. It is during the final component of the PLC+ framework that this is mapped out for both the teachers and the learners. Again, once we identify who did not benefit from our teaching, we must collaboratively develop a different way of approaching our instruction, whether through the enhancement of Tier 1 instruction or the implementation of supplemental and intensive interventions.

> Creating and implementing a multitiered system of support such as RTI is complex but worth the effort.

Creating and implementing a multitiered system of support such as RTI is complex but worth the effort. It's complex because, prior to the PLC+ model, there were no systems that systematically assimilated this process into common planning or PLC+ discussions. Devoting time to the question of who benefited and who did not is worth the effort, because this allows us to make the right decisions at the right time to maximize the benefit to student learning.

MEETING THE NEEDS OF ALL LEARNERS

In the previous section, we mentioned that RTI was not louder, longer, and more of the same. At the same time, we highlighted that as students progress toward the learning intentions, learning should not be compromised. We should consider adjusting the rate of learning and the instruction. Furthermore, are there language and social-emotional interventions that would support students' learning progress? Let's get right to the point: In a classroom of 33 students, all of whom demonstrated different levels of performance and growth, how is Ms. Lancaster supposed to meet the needs of each learner? And to continue this very transparent and direct line of questioning, is it okay to simply leave the upper right quadrant of learners (Figure 6.11) to fend for themselves?

FIGURE 6.11   **Students in the High-Growth and High-Achievement Quadrant**

After all, they are Williams Elementary School's high achievement–high growth learners.

Bringing together a collaborative network of colleagues that are committed to providing each learner *at least* a year's worth of growth in a year's worth of schooling is the foundation for ensuring all learners have equity of access and opportunity to learn. The use of the words *at least* is intentional. For some learners, a year's worth of growth is not sufficient. To close achievement gaps, learning needs to be accelerated for some of our students.

> RTI is not louder, longer, and more of the same.

To ensure that all learners benefit from our instruction, the focus of this chapter and final component of the PLC+ framework, we must modify learning experiences and tasks to meet the specific needs of all learners (social, emotional, and cognitive). To ensure that learners will benefit from instruction, without compromising the targeted learning, Ms. Lancaster and her team must differentiate instruction by developing tasks that allow them to adjust the level of difficulty while maintaining the level of complexity expected in the learning intention. In other words, the learning environment must be inclusive of all learners, at all spots on the learning progression. Where better to have this discussion and plan out this next step in the learning process than the PLC+ collaborative team meeting. Let's unpack this a bit more.

THE PROFESSIONAL LEARNING OF PLC+

Before we move forward in the conversation, we want to take another moment and look at the *professional learning* aspect of a PLC+. We have done this in previous chapters, but we cannot overlook the question about where professional learning comes into play during this final part of the framework. As we engage in answering the question "Who benefited and who did not benefit?' our comfort level or ability to truly know how to respond to this benefit analysis may be hindered by our own pedagogical content knowledge, not to mention our level of cultural proficiency. Say, for example, one of our team members is not aware of how to modify a task for speakers of other languages or learners that need additional scaffolding with some aspect of the content. This calls for targeted professional learning to close this member's pedagogical content knowledge gap. Although team members can support their colleagues in this journey, having the capacity to meet the needs of learners now and in the future is part of the individual and collective efficacy of the PLC+.

There may be times when targeted professional learning is needed to close a group member's pedagogical content knowledge gap.

Down the hallway, Michael Martin and his PLC+ are preparing to assign a performance task that integrates science, reading, and writing. "Before we assign this task, we need to look at who has and has not benefited from instruction, so that we can make the necessary adjustments that will allow all learners to have access to this experience. Plus, the modifications will help close the learning gap for some of our students while at the same time extending the learning of those demonstrating a high level of performance and growth," says Mr. Martin. As Ms. Lancaster did with her PLC+, Mr. Martin has used assessment data to address the question of benefit. What he and his PLC+ are adamant about is ensuring that learning moves forward for all students: "We don't want to stop learning new content for those needing additional support or delay learning for those that have demonstrated proficiency or mastery. Instead, we want to keep moving forward in learning by making modifications to our instruction."

Next week, learners will be assigned the task of creating two different drums using different materials for each drum. In cooperative learning groups, they must be sure that the drums make different sounds. When finished, all groups will play their drums for the class and explain what materials were used. The final component of the task is to write a descriptive paragraph about what causes sound.

However, one of Mr. Martin's colleagues remarks that she has no idea how to make this happen with her class. They decide to use this time to talk through the modification of this task while at the same time selecting professional resources that will support their own professional learning. After much conversation, they map out the following plan, which uses flexible grouping and adjusts the level of support for each group of learners.

- One group will be provided images of drums, guiding research questions about drums, video resources, leveled readers for research on drums, and sentence frames for the writing component.

- A second group will receive guiding research questions, leveled readers, a choice of graphic organizers, and guiding questions for the writing component.

- A third group will receive guiding research questions, a selection of reading materials, and guiding questions for the writing component.

- A final group will be expected to do independent research on drums and to self-select their reading materials. They will receive no scaffolding for the writing component.

The conversations in Ms. Lancaster's PLC+, much like the conversations in Mr. Martin's PLC+, made the modification of learning experiences possible. From Daniel to Eduardo, Ms. Lancaster recognized who was and was not benefiting from her instruction and responded to this information. She brought this information forward and drew on the individual and collective efficacy of her colleagues to generate ideas about how to meet the needs of learners, whether they were or were not making gains. "I don't want to ignore those learners that are demonstrating a high rate of learning and a high level of performance. I do not believe that I can radically impact student learning by making my learners do a lot more work."

Learners who have met or exceed learning expectations should not be rewarded with an automatic increase in difficulty. Reading extra-long text, writing essay after essay after essay, practicing hundreds of division problems, or writing the definitions of hundreds of science terms will not extend the thinking of learners. Furthermore, relegating learners to a day filled with the rote memorization and rehearsal of content they are not learning at a preferred pace or level of performance will not close their learning gap. Keeping in mind that asking students to engage in a task, assignment, or strategy that is far too complex or not complex enough for their current need can also reduce the benefit on student learning and engagement. Instead, we should use data to balance difficulty and complexity in addressing the benefit of our teaching. Continuing to monitor progress or engage in ongoing assessment will allow Ms. Lancaster and

> Learners who have met or exceed learning expectations should not be rewarded with an automatic increase in difficulty.

her PLC+ team to keep adjusting the level of complexity or difficulty. Our learners need to experience a *wide range* of tasks if we are going to identify which instructional approach provides maximum benefit to their learning. They need opportunities to work with their teacher, with their peers, and independently so that they develop the social, emotional, and academic skills necessary to continue to learn on their own.

CONCLUSION

When considering the reply to the question "Who benefited and who did not benefit?" PLC+ teams focus tightly on identifying patterns that reveal themselves among particular groups of learners, patterns that may suggest underlying issues or institutional barriers to learning. Once we identify patterns and analyze data, PLC+ teams demonstrate self-efficacy and collective efficacy and build credibility when we engage in an equity audit, determine tiered systems of support, and ultimately modify instruction to address the barriers to learning.

This chapter provides examples of facilitated discussions and actions with teams where honest, candid, and at times uncomfortable conversations happen through data analysis to assess teaching and learning in classrooms. We designed the PLC+ model to honor teacher learning and to support teams as we address barriers to learning and ensure that every student is learning, not by chance, but by design. In order to remove barriers to learning, PLC+ teams are prepared to use their collective efficacy to collaboratively learn together different methods of approaching instruction. It is important to note that many teams lose their steam at this juncture. We need to support an environment where there *can* be a focus on learning by providing PLC+ teams with time to do this work, and to focus that time on the right work.

The PLC+ model provides teams with a structure to build the capacity to meet the needs of learners now and in the future. The following table lists processes and approaches that are highlighted in this chapter that support the four core values of PLC+ teams. These provide guidance to our teams as we determine who benefited and who did not, and as we plan to respond and learn from quality professional learning to meet the learning needs of all of our students. Responding to this question in a team builds individual and collective efficacy and develops the capacity that reaches beyond individual teachers in their classrooms and across the school.

EQUITY	As mentioned in this chapter, it is important for PLC+ team members to look at trends and patterns in both growth and achievement. Are there common characteristics of learners not experiencing growth and/or achievement? This could support establishing supplemental and intensive interventions to provide equity of access and opportunity for all learners. • How does your PLC+ currently look at student-level trends in your progress and achievement data? • In what ways does your PLC+ ensure that all students are not only reaching adequate achievement levels, but also demonstrating growth? • How could an equity audit support student learning in your school or classroom?
HIGH EXPECTATIONS	We should all operate under the strongly held expectation that learners will both grow and achieve in their learning. In addition to setting high expectations through purposefully designed learning tasks, we must also expect that these tasks will produce both significant gains in student learning and, eventually, high achievement. Reflecting on who did and who did not benefit will maintain our expectations for both growth and achievement, but at the same time will increase our understanding of who is and who is not making those gains. *And why they aren't.* • How can the growth versus achievement grid work within your PLC+ support equity in expectations? • What approaches does your PLC+ currently use to determine whether learners need supplemental or intensive supports? • What is the link between student background or demographic characteristics and expectations of their learning growth and achievement?
INDIVIDUAL AND COLLECTIVE EFFICACY	The learning aspect of a PLC+ builds our efficacy in responding to the equity audit and knowing how to plan, design, and implement both supplemental and intensive interventions. The recognition of those learners that did not benefit from instruction should prompt our PLC+ to engage in professional learning around supporting all learners. Where there is not immediate expertise in addressing a common challenge or problem of practice, there must be professional learning that builds that expertise—and thus enhances the efficacy of the individual members and the collective PLC+. • In what ways do you currently engage in new learning with your PLC+? • How could development of pedagogical content knowledge for specific groups of learners within your PLC+ support development of individual and collective efficacy?

(Continued)

(Continued)

| ACTIVATION | As we have said before, effectively analyzing student performance data within a PLC+ can oftentimes be a challenge. Looking at who did and who did not benefit makes this all the more challenging. When we look at the growth versus achievement grid through the lens of impact, we must work collaboratively to ensure our conversations are focused on what to do about those learners not benefiting from instruction. Strong activation of such challenging conversations is paramount. |

- What do you think are key attributes of an activator who can facilitate a PLC+ discussion where teachers feel okay to be vulnerable?
- What is the link between effective activation and genuine reflection?

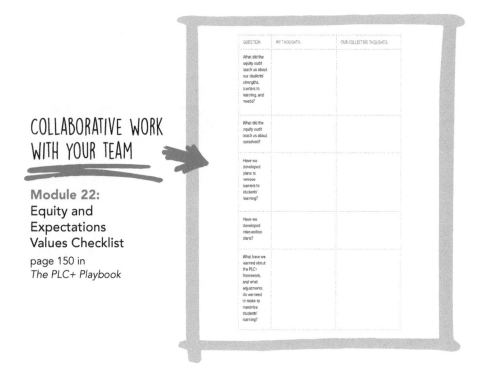

COLLABORATIVE WORK
WITH YOUR TEAM

Module 22:
Equity and
Expectations
Values Checklist

page 150 in
The PLC+ Playbook

ACTIVATE LEARNING FOR MYSELF AND OTHERS CHECKLIST

Student learning needs drive adult learning needs. Once teams understand where students are now in their learning journey, teams need to take a step back to reflect on their personal learning. Are there any adult learning needs that must be met to best be able to support student learning? As already discussed, the + in the PLC+ is you, and so it is important to recognize learning for teachers is a constant. Given that you want to move student learning forward, what learning do you (or your team) need to accomplish to ensure that all students are successful?

WHAT TRENDS DID WE NOTICE ABOUT STUDENTS WHO DID OR DID NOT BENEFIT?	WHAT ARE MY LEARNING NEEDS SO I CAN MEET MY STUDENTS' LEARNING NEEDS? What strategies might I need to learn more about?	WHAT LEARNING WILL I ENGAGE IN TO MEET MY LEARNING NEEDS? What will I do on my own? What can I do with colleagues?

COLLECTIVE EFFICACY CHECKLIST

Teams that are empowered to make decisions, take action, communicate clearly, and hold themselves accountable for their efforts manifest high degrees of collective teacher efficacy (CTE). Use the checklist below to gauge and monitor the actions that will follow your work about the fifth guiding question, "Who benefited and who did not benefit?"

QUESTION	MY THOUGHTS	OUR COLLECTIVE THOUGHTS
How confident are we feeling as a team in our instructional abilities?		
How confident are we feeling in removing barriers to student learning?		
How confident are we feeling in our ability to design and deliver effective intervention systems?		
What mastery experiences did we have that built the collective efficacy of our team?		

COLLABORATIVE WORK WITH YOUR TEAM

Module 22:
Activate Learning for Myself and Others Checklist

page 151 in
The PLC+ Playbook

COLLABORATIVE WORK WITH YOUR TEAM

Module 22:
Collective Efficacy Checklist

page 152 in
The PLC+ Playbook

The NEXT QUESTION in the PLC+ FRAMEWORK

Over the past six chapters, we have presented a framework, driven by five guiding questions, for the planning and implementation of student learning, as well as our own professional learning, via numerous approaches from engaging in research to microteaching and classroom observations. The five questions are as follows:

1. **Where are we going?**

2. **Where are we now?**

3. **How do we move learning forward?**

4. **What did we learn today?**

5. **Who benefited and who did not benefit?**

We have taken an in-depth look at each of the five questions associated with the **plus** framework, and noted that the *plus* in the PLC+ is you.

By looking over the shoulders of several individuals in PLC+ collaborative team meetings, we witnessed teachers from across all grade levels and content areas use these five questions to maximize student learning in their classrooms. They also used these questions to drive their own professional learning. We witnessed these teams unpack the meaning and intent of each of the five questions and engage in dialogue around teaching and learning in their classrooms. The conversations were informed by four fundamental values: equity, strong activation, high expectations, and individual and collective efficacy. Wrestling with the difficult conversations that come with discussions about teaching and learning is critical and unavoidable if we are ever to move the needle and increase the learning

Video 8
Introduction to Chapter 7

resources.corwin.com/
plcplus

outcomes for all students. As each PLC+ team member brings his or her own beliefs, mindsets, and behaviors to the team meeting, how does the team, as a whole, address and respond to potential barriers in the dialogue that could impede the professional learning and student learning in their classrooms? Our response comprises the following crosscutting values, which drive the work within the five questions:

1. We must keep the **equity** of access and opportunity for learning at the forefront of each PLC+ collaborative team meeting.

2. We must ensure that **activation** of the dialogue is provoked by the five questions and is carried out in such a way that the work of the PLC+ is accelerated, not hindered or impeded.

3. We must develop learning experiences that make our **expectations** for learning clear to all students.

4. And finally, the collaborative work of the PLC+ should leverage our **individual efficacy** into **collective teacher efficacy**.

AFTER THE FIFTH QUESTION

However, the effectiveness of the PLC+ framework, the true manifestation of the plus where instruction is now part of the equation, does not come from a series of meetings. Let's return to Kathy Garber's PLC+, first introduced in Chapter 2. As you recall, Ms. Garber explicitly stated that "our PLC+ team meetings are part of a continual process. We never finish. As a team, we circle back around and use the five essential questions as an iterative process." And that is exactly one of two final messages we want to convey here and emphasize as we conclude this book. The effectiveness of the PLC+ framework is the iterative nature of the questions, as well as the characteristic of each question to engage teachers in dialogue about teaching and learning in the hallways of the school, in the classrooms where we teach, and in the parking lot when we linger to continue a conversation with a colleague. The five guiding questions become metacognitive scripts that teachers ask themselves regularly, even when they are not with colleagues.

When we first met Ms. Garber and her professional learning community, they had gathered the necessary curriculum documents to engage in their work around where they were going and where they wanted to take their learners. "We spent several days during our planning period and, at times, lunch period dialoguing back and forth about what really were the essential knowledge, skills, and understandings that we wanted our learners to get. Sometimes we have to remind ourselves to talk about other things." However, Ms. Garber points out that this initial step, even if this is not completed in one setting, is essential in determining where their learners are now, the essence of the second question.

"Once we know where we are going, we spend time developing initial assessments that will inform us, and our learners, about their current position in the learning progression." Ms. Garber's PLC+ team works together to develop initial assessments of student learning through the collection of work samples, student interviews, and initial assessments. "We try very hard to avoid initial assessments that chain students to their desks at the start of each unit, responding to standardized-like test items. This is a terrible way to start new learning. We try to find other ways to elicit student ideas and student thinking, like using anticipation guides."

From here, Ms. Garber and her team use that information to strategically plan the learning experiences that move learning forward. One colleague notes that "we hear so much about evidence-based practices and how we should use them each and every day. This requires us to be very purposeful in the ones we use, to truly understand how to apply them in our classroom practice, and to ensure we are using the right strategy at the right time." In addition, Ms. Garber and her team set up an evidence-gathering plan that will help them address the next question. They collect and analyze data regularly and meet often to talk about their findings. One member states that "for us, the selecting and planning for ways to move learning forward is the most fluid conversation in the framework. We hear about or read about something new and then share it among ourselves at all times during the day. In fact, until we have a robust collection of

> The five guiding questions become metacognitive scripts that teachers ask themselves regularly, even when they are not with colleagues.

evidence like student work samples, exit tickets, and journal responses, we keep the conversation on ways to move learning forward. We regularly sit down and look at the evidence in more formal ways, but we are collecting evidence to use formatively all of the time."

When uncovering what they have learned about their students, Ms. Garber and her team return back to the learning intentions, success criteria, and initial assessment data associated with this particular content. "Now we have something to look over and compare with each student's starting point," says Ms. Garber. What is most noticeable about this aspect of her team's PLC+ work is that their collective efficacy both in using the framework and in teaching and learning allows them to naturally move from the question of "What did we learn today?" and into "Who benefited who did not benefit?" from their teaching. "Once we became comfortable as a team, overcoming several of the barriers in this type of work, we naturally moved to the conversation about who did and did not benefit."

At this point in the PLC+ framework, the iterative nature of the questions comes to life.

At this point in the PLC+ framework, the iterative nature of the questions comes to life. In their dialogue about who did and did not benefit, Ms. Garber and her team begin to explore the evidence that points to learners that did not benefit from their instruction and the potential commonalities among these learners. "We naturally begin to talk about the learning experiences and whether or not the learning experiences provided students who did not perform well the same quality as those who did perform well. When we look at the growth-versus-achievement grid through this lens, we must work collaboratively to ensure our conversations are focused on what to do next for those learners not benefiting from instruction. The discomfort that sometimes slides into this part of the framework is so worth it in the end."

As Ms. Garber and her team continue in this conversation, other members of the team begin to rework the learning intentions and success criteria for the upcoming days: "Okay, let's adjust our learning intentions and success criteria for the next week to align with where we see a need for additional teaching and learning. We have to readjust our progressions just a bit." Her PLC+ team recognizes that there are gaps in learning that must be filled to ensure that learners can eventually meet the expectations of the standard, while at the same time providing rigorous learning tasks for those learners moving forward at a more rapid pace: "Okay, let's map out how we are going to move learning forward for each group of our learners." And the process continues.

This is the same experience that was reported by Rachel Lancaster and her first-grade PLC+, Gina Johnston and her fourth-grade PLC+, Mike Leonard and his eighth-grade PLC+, Janice Baker and her high school PLC+, Judy Howser and her high school PLC+, and Megan Andrews and her creative arts PLC+ in previous chapters. To quote Ms. Garber once more, "Our PLC+ team meetings are part of a continual process. We never finish. As a team, we circle back around and use the five essential questions to formulate our next common challenge."

> "Our PLC+ team meetings are part of a continual process. We never finish. As a team, we circle back around and use the five essential questions to formulate our next common challenge."

Recognizing that the PLC+ framework is an iterative process removes the restricted thinking that number of meetings corresponds with number of questions. For example, holding the first PLC+ meeting does not mean you only focus on the first question and that you must "finish" the first question by the end of the first meeting because your second PLC+ meeting is reserved for the second question. Instead, Ms. Garber and her colleagues may spend two or three PLC+ meetings answering the question "Where are we going?" For example, if a particular set of skills and content is difficult and complex, the team may need to devote more time to the development of learning intentions, success criteria, learning progressions, and their own professional learning around those skills and content. And as we have said before, these conversations may continue in the hallway, teachers' workroom, or parking lot.

BEYOND A SINGLE PLC+

The second message we want to convey in the closing of this book looks beyond Ms. Garber and her PLC+. The PLC+ framework leverages the individual efficacy of teachers into collective efficacy for a grade-level team or content area team. However, the efficacy of each individual PLC+ can leverage this collective efficacy to engage an entire school or school district. The power in the PLC+

framework—the effectiveness of the iterative process stoked by the five questions—comes from the very nature of collective efficacy. As colleagues witness the success of Ms. Garber and her PLC+ team, these vicarious experiences, along with social persuasion and the affective state of Ms. Garber's team, will make the PLC+ framework contagious to others in the building. Furthermore, the way Ms. Garber and her team utilize the dynamic of teacher credibility will continue to enlarge their sphere of influence from classroom leaders to instructional leaders to teacher leaders. Success breeds success.

This is the ultimate goal of the PLC+ framework. This should be the way we do business in our classrooms, schools, and school districts. Using the five questions to facilitate dialogue about teaching and learning for all learners should be the culture of every classroom, school, and district; *plus*, the climate makes it feel right.

REFERENCES

Abrams, J. (2016). *Hard conversations unpacked: The whos, the whens, and the what-ifs*. Thousand Oaks, CA: Corwin.

Ainsworth, L. (2014). *Common formative assessments 2.0: How teacher teams intentionally align standards, instruction, and assessment*. Thousand Oaks, CA: Corwin.

Almarode, J., & Vandas, K. (2018). Clarity for learning: *Five essential practices that empower students and teachers*. Thousand Oaks, CA: Corwin.

Atkins, S., & Murphy, K. (1994). Reflective practice. *Nursing Standard, 8*(39), 49–54.

Bandura, A. (1982). Self-efficacy mechanism in human agency. *American Psychologist, 37*(2), 122–147.

Bandura, A. (1986). *Social foundations of thought and action: A social cognitive theory*. Englewood Cliffs, NJ: Prentice-Hall.

Bandura, A. (1997). *Self-efficacy: The exercise of control*. New York: W. H. Freeman.

Boud, D., Cohen, R., & Sampson, J. (1999). Peer learning and assessment. *Assessment & Evaluation in Higher Education, 24*(4), 413.

Boud, D., Keogh, R., & Walker, D. (1985). What is reflection in learning? In D. Boud, R. Keogh, & D. Walker (Eds.), *Reflection: Turning experience into learning* (pp. 85–90). New York: Nichols.

Brown, L. T., Mohr, K. A. J., Wilcox, B. R., & Barre, T. S. (2017). Effects of dyad reading and text difficulty on third-graders' reading achievement. (2017). *Journal of Educational Research, 111*(5), 541–553.

Bryk, A., Camburn, E., & Louis, K. S. (1999). Professional community in Chicago elementary schools: Facilitating factors and organizational consequences. *Educational Administration Quarterly, 35*, 751–781.

Charner-Laird, M., Ippolito, J., & Dobbs, C. L. (2016). The roles of teacher leaders in guiding PLCs focused on disciplinary literacy. *Journal of School Leadership, 26*, 975–1001.

Choppin, J. (2011). The impact of professional noticing on teachers' adaptations of challenging tasks. *Mathematical Thinking & Learning, 13*(3), 175–197.

City, E. A., Elmore, R. F., Fiarman, S. E., & Teitel, L. (2009). *Instructional rounds in education. A network approach to improving teaching and learning*. Cambridge, MA: Harvard Education Press.

Cockerell, L. (2008). *Creating magic: 10 common sense leadership strategies from a life at Disney*. New York, NY: Currency.

Colton, A., Langer, G., & Goff, L. (2015). *Collaborative analysis of student learning: Professional learning that promotes success for all*. Thousand Oaks, CA: Corwin.

Deno, S. L. (1987). Curriculum-based measurement. *Teaching Exceptional Children, 20*(1), 40–42.

Donohoo, J. (2017). *Collective efficacy: How educators' beliefs impact student learning*. Thousand Oaks, CA: Sage.

DuFour, R., DuFour, R., Eaker, R., & Many, T. (2010). *Learning by doing: A handbook for professional learning communities at work*. Bloomington, IN: Solution Tree Press.

Education Trust. (2016). *Checking in update: More assignments from real classrooms*. Washington, DC: Author. Retrieved from https://1k9gl1yevnf-p2lpq1dhrqe17-wpengine.netdna-ssl.com/wp-content/uploads/2014/09/CheckingInUpdate_AssignmentsFromRealClassrooms_EdTrust_April2016.pdf

Education Trust. (2018). *Checking in: Are math assignments measuring up?* Retrieved from https://1k9gl1yevnfp2lpq1dhrqe17-wpengine.netdna-ssl.com/wp-content/uploads/2014/09/CheckingIn_MATH-ANALYSIS_FINAL_5.pdf

Engel, M., Claessens, A., & Finch, M. A. (2013). Teaching students what they already know? The (mis)alignment between mathematics instructional content and student knowledge in kindergarten. *Educational Evaluation and Policy Analysis, 35*(2), 157–178.

Fisher, D., & Frey, N. (2004). *Inclusive urban schools*. Baltimore, MD: Paul H. Brookes.

Fisher, D., & Frey, N. (2010). *Enhancing RTI: How to ensure success with effective classroom instruction and intervention*. Alexandria, VA: ASCD.

Fisher, D., Frey, N., Amador, O., & Assof, J. (2018). *The teacher clarity playbook*. Thousand Oaks, CA: Corwin.

Fisher, D., Frey, N., & Hattie, J. (2016). *Visible learning for literacy, grades K–12: Implementing the practices that work best to accelerate student learning*. Thousand Oaks, CA: Corwin.

Garrett, R., & Hong, G. (2016). Impacts of grouping and time on the math learning of language minority kindergartners. *Educational Evaluation & Policy Analysis, 38*(2), 222–244.

Gibson, S. A., & Ross, P. (2016). Teachers' professional noticing. *Theory Into Practice, 55*(3), 180–188.

Goddard, R. D., & Goddard, Y. L. (2001). A multilevel analysis of teacher and collective efficacy. *Teaching and Teacher Education, 17*, 807–818.

Goddard, R., Hoy, W., & Woolfolk Hoy, A. (2004). Collective efficacy beliefs: Theoretical developments, empirical evidence, and future directions. *Educational Researcher, 33*(3), 3–13.

Hattie, J. (2009). *Visible learning: A synthesis of over 800 meta-analyses relating to achievement*. New York, NY: Routledge.

Hattie, J. (2012). *Visible learning for teachers: Maximizing impact on learning*. New York, NY: Routledge.

Hord, S. (2004). Professional learning communities: An overview. In S. Hord (Ed.), *Learning together, leading together: Changing schools through professional learning communities* (pp. 5–14). New York, NY: Teachers College Press.

Horn, I. S., & Little, J. W. (2010). Attending to problems of practice: Routines and resources for professional learning in teachers' workplace interactions. *American Educational Research Journal, 47*(1), 181–217.

Hwang, J., Choi, K. M., Bae, Y., & Shin, D. H. (2018). Do teachers' instructional practices moderate equity in mathematical and scientific literacy? An investigation of the PISA 2012 and 2015. *International Journal of Science & Mathematics Education, 16*(1), 25–45.

Lai, M., Wilson, A., McNaughton, S., & Hsiao, S. (2014). Improving achievement in secondary schools: Impact of a literacy project on reading comprehension and secondary school qualifications. *Reading Research Quarterly, 49*(3), 305–334.

Learning Forward. (2017). *Select learning designs*. Retrieved from https://learningforward.org/standards/learning-designs

Lindsey, D. B., Jungwirth, L. D., Pahl, J. V. N. C., & Lindsey, R. B. (2009). *Culturally proficient learning communities: Confronting inequities through collaborative curiosity*. Thousand Oaks, CA: Corwin.

Little, J. W. (1987). Teachers as colleagues. In V. Richardson-Koehler (Ed.), *Educators' handbook: A research perspective* (pp. 491–518). New York, NY: Longman.

Louis, K. S., & Kruse, S. D. (1995). *Professionalism and community: Perspectives on reforming urban schools*. Thousand Oaks, CA: Corwin.

MacDonald, E. (2013). *The skillful team leader: A resource for overcoming hurdles to professional learning for student achievement*. Thousand Oaks, CA: Corwin.

Marzano, R. J. (2007). *The art and science of teaching: A comprehensive framework for effective instruction*. Alexandria, VA: ASCD.

National Governors Association Center for Best Practices & Council of Chief State School Officers. (2010). *Common Core State Standards for mathematics*. Washington DC: National Governors Association Center for Best Practices & Council of Chief State School Officers.

Okes, D. (1999). *Root cause analysis: The core of problem solving and corrective action*. Milwaukee, WI: American Society for Quality.

Opfer, V. D., & Pedder, D. (2011). Conceptualizing teacher professional learning. *Review of Educational Research, 81*, 376–407.

Palincsar, A. S., & Brown, A. (1984). Reciprocal teaching of comprehension-fostering and comprehension-monitoring activities. *Cognition and Instruction, 1*(2), 117–175.

Payne, K., Niemi, L., & Doris, J. M. (2018, March 27). How to think about implicit bias. *Scientific American*. Retrieved from https://www.scientificamerican.com/article/how-to-think-about-implicit-bias/

Popham, W. J. (2008). *Transformative assessment*. Alexandria, VA: ASCD.

Rosenholtz, S. J. (1989). *Teachers' workplace: The social organization of schools*. New York, NY: Longman.

Schlichte, J., Yssel, N., & Merbler, J. (2005). Pathways to burnout: Case studies in teacher isolation and alienation. *Preventing School Failure, 50*(1), 35–40.

Shaw, D. (2017). Accomplished teaching: Using video recorded micro-teaching discourse to build candidate teaching competencies. *Journal of Interactive Learning Research, 28*(2), 161–180.

Stoll, L., Bolam, R., McMahon, A., Wallace, M., & Thomas, S. (2006). Professional learning communities: A review of the literature. *Journal of Educational Change, 7*, 221–258.

Timperley, H. (2011). *Revitalizing the power of professional learning*. New York, NY: McGraw-Hill.

Timperley, H., Kaser, L., & Halbert, J. (2014, April). *A framework for transforming learning in schools: Innovation and the spiral of inquiry*. Seminar series 234. Melbourne, Australia: Center for Strategic Education.

Tomlinson, C. (2001). *How to differentiate instruction in mixed-ability classrooms* (2nd ed.). Alexandria, VA: ASCD.

Tschannen-Moran, M., & Barr, M. (2004). Fostering student learning: The relationship of collective teacher efficacy and student achievement. *Leadership and Policy in Schools, 3*(3), 189–209.

Tschannen-Moran, M., Woolfolk Hoy, A., & Hoy, W. K. (1998). Teacher efficacy: Its meaning and measure. *Review of Educational Research, 68*(2), 202–248.

Valencia, R. R. (n.d.). Deficit thinking paradigm. In J. A. Banks (Ed.), *Encyclopedia of diversity in education*. doi:http://dx.doi.org/10.4135/9781452218533.n191

Vangrieken, K., Meredith, C., Packer, T., & Kyndt, E. (2017). Teacher communities as a context for professional development: A systematic review. *Teacher and Teacher Education, 61*, 47–59.

Vescio, V., Ross, D., & Adams, A. (2008). A review of research on the impact of professional learning communities on teaching practice and student learning. *Teaching and Teacher Education: An International Journal of Research and Studies, 24*(1), 80–91.

Webb, N. L. (2005, November 17). *Alignment, depth of knowledge, and change.* Presentation at the 50th Annual Meeting of the Florida Educational Research Association, Miami, FL. Retrieved from http://facstaff.wcer.wisc.edu/normw/MIAMI%20FLORIDA%20FINAL%20slides%2011-15-05.pdf

Wenger, E., McDermott, R., & Snyder, W. M. (2002). *A guide to managing knowledge: Cultivating communities of practice.* Boston, MA: Harvard Business School Press.

Wiliam, D. (2011). *Embedded formative assessment.* Bloomington, IN: Solution Tree Press.

Woolfolk, A. E., Winne, P. H., & Perry, N. E. (2011). *Educational psychology.* New York, NY: Pearson.

Yopp, H. (1995). A test for assessing phonemic awareness in young children. *The Reading Teacher, 49,* 20–29.

INDEX

A SAGE Publishing Company

Helping educators make the greatest impact

CORWIN HAS ONE MISSION: to enhance education through intentional professional learning.

We build long-term relationships with our authors, educators, clients, and associations who partner with us to develop and continuously improve the best evidence-based practices that establish and support lifelong learning.

3 Ways to get started with PLC+

The **PLC+ framework** is designed to refresh current collaborative structures and support teachers' decision making in the context of individual and collective efficacy, expectations, equity, and the activation of their own learning.

1

Watch the PLC+ Webinar

Preview the PLC+ framework with thought leaders Douglas Fisher and Nancy Frey.

To view the webinar, visit corwin.com/PLCWebinar

2

Attend an Event

Attendees will walk away with a better understanding of the PLC+ framework's potential impact, steps for implementation, and how to build individual and collective efficacy as well as teacher credibility.

For more information, visit corwin.com/PLCInstitutes

3

Meet With a Senior Professional Learning Advisor

Our Senior Professional Learning Advisors will help assess your current PLC structures or discuss options for implementation if your school is new to PLCs. Our customizable PLC+ PD Series ensures better decisions and greater impact by design.

For more information, visit corwin.com/PLCPD

CORWIN PLC+